# ALREADY HOME

## CONFRONTING THE TRAUMA OF ADOPTION

### HOWARD FREDERICK IBACH

ISBN: 979-8-9892923-0-1 (Hardcover edition)
979-8-9892923-1-8 (Paperback edition)
979-8-9892923-2-5 (Ebook edition)

*For Martha Joyce and Harold Frederick Ibach, MD, my parents*

*and*

*Irene, Berlon, Susan, Jayne, Tony, John, and Chip*

*and*

*Adoptees, adoptees-to-be, those who want to adopt and mothers who gift their infant for adoption*

"I wanted to go on an immense journey, to travel night and day into the unknown until, forgetting my old self, I came into possession of a new self, one that I might have missed on my previous travels. But the first step was beyond me."

~Mark Strand

# PROLOGUE

George Watson was the father of my life, but he was not my father. His actions more than sixty-four years ago set in motion the events that led to my birth. He killed a man so that I might live. What his intentions were on the day he took a life, I do not know. But I know the result.

Is it macabre to say that I am grateful to a man who committed such a deed? It gives me no pleasure. Sometimes I am bewildered by the consequences of his actions. When I learned about George Watson, I was flooded with emotions and numbed. Sometimes I felt and sometimes I did not feel, all at the same time, as if I were standing beside myself impassively watching this other me feel anger and confusion. What was clear is that without George Watson, I would not be here.

THE MAN GEORGE WATSON killed was named Eulo Small, Jr., but everyone called him Junior. His wife was Irene Small. Junior died on November 4, 1955, only weeks before their third wedding anniversary.

The spot where Junior died resides as a crisp image in my mind because I have stood on that ground, I have surveyed the landscape. He perished in a violent head-on collision near what locals called the Jones Dairy on a quiet stretch of road outside a hamlet called Nichols in South Carolina, population at the time around four hundred.

Today, the scene looks like a Hollywood movie set that was abandoned decades earlier and left to rot. Three structures squat on the arid land that was once a working dairy farm: two crumbling outbuildings and a lonely silo scalped of its cone-shaped top, its remaining circumference strangled by a dead creeping vine. The dairy failed in the 1960s according to locals. It has sat idle ever since, slowly disintegrating, scrubbed of color and all remnants of its former life.

Junior's obituary offered few details, but my mind needed little fodder to imagine the events that unfolded that day in 1955.

It began with George Watson, the antagonist and catalyst of my version of this story. He swayed drunkenly as he stepped up onto the eighteen-wheel logging truck. He reached for the door handle, but it was locked. He fumbled for the keys and dropped them. They clanked loudly on the metal between his feet. He bent to retrieve them, lurching unsteadily. He stood upright, or tried to, then forced his eyes to focus on the keys in his hands. He found what he thought was the right one and attempted to insert it into the lock, missing several times.

George Watson's logging truck was loaded. So was he. It was not his first liquid lunch, but he was not concerned. He knew the route.

Once on the road, he moved his truck slowly through the gears. In his condition, he moved unsteadily. Soon he turned onto Nichols Highway, outside the town of the same name in northeast South Carolina.

Nichols Highway was a two-lane country road paved in faded asphalt with a broken white center line. Nothing about it said "highway," neither today nor back in 1955 when George, drunk as he was so often before, got into his truck. There were few posted speed limits, fewer patrolling police cars.

The eighteen-wheeler gained speed and soon George approached a soft curve in the highway. He was nearing a familiar landmark, the Jones Dairy.

It was here, in sight of the dairy—a busy farm back then, alive with activity, ripe with the smell of cows and manure, chickens clucking, dogs barking—that George lost control of his eighteen-wheel logging truck. It slid slowly, inexorably across the broken white line. He probably did not realize it was happening.

No one will ever know how the driver of the on-coming vehicle reacted at that moment. There was probably some reaction, but it arrived in vain, witnessed only by the old silo at the Jones Dairy. Today the silo leans away from the highway, as if it were still turned away from the accident in horror. But someone must have heard what happened as the eighteen-wheeler slammed into the vehicle. According to Junior's obituary, his car was traveling at about forty-five miles an hour. He died instantly.

They say an eighteen-wheeler always wins the argument. George Watson walked away, unharmed. It was 2:30 p.m. on November 4, 1955. A Friday. Junior was twenty-eight years old when George killed him.

It was not hard to imagine the scene along Nichols Highway more than sixty years ago, when the Jones Dairy became the unwanted center of attention. There was no 9-1-1, no cell phones, but someone must have called the police, had an ambulance dispatched. George Watson was not arrested, but he had to appear at an inquest and a court hearing, where his actions were determined to have been an accident. That much was in Junior's obituary.

After a tour as an Army first lieutenant in Korea, Junior settled his family in Mullins, his hometown, a mile or two down the road from Nichols. He was laid to rest in a nearby cemetery. A little more than three years earlier, he had met a woman, Irene, at Ft. Dix in New Jersey. She was an Army nurse, a second lieutenant. They fell in love, married, and had two daughters, Susan, and Jayne.

George Watson made Irene a widow with young children on that November day in 1955. She knew him—not personally, but by reputation. After the accident that killed her husband, she had heard the stories about George: that he bragged about being stone drunk, about getting off scot-free. She knew he was guilty. She called him a murderer.

In all likelihood, George Watson is dead now. It is probable that he lived out his life indifferent to the consequences of the fatal accident he caused on Nichols Highway.

George Watson had no history that I could uncover before he slammed his eighteen-wheel logging truck into Junior's car. Nor could I find anything about him after the accident. He was nothing more to me than an apparition who performed his role, then disappeared. He was a bit player in every way imaginable, but also one who changed history. Not of nations, nor of communities, but certainly in the lives of one family. And mine, too.

In Irene's grief at the death of her husband, Junior, she met another man. He consoled her, offered her his shoulder for comfort, and became intimate with her and she with him. Soon Irene was pregnant. She gave birth to a boy on November 22, 1956, more than a year after Junior was killed by George Watson. The day after the boy was born, Irene turned him over for adoption. Twenty-six days later, he went home with Martha and Harold Ibach.

That boy was me.

# 1

One morning in May 2015, I took the first step to find my birth mother while at Gold's Gym in Hollywood, although I did not know it at the time.

I was standing between an abs and a pectoral machine, with the sounds of guys grunting, metal clanking on metal and loud dance music blaring over speakers attached to the ceiling. A buddy was sharing his thoughts on couple therapy.

"Yeah, it's worth it," said Bill, a freelance trainer I'd met three years earlier. He was a regular at the gym and had been training clients there for twenty-five years. He was in his early sixties but appeared much younger. At six-two, his biceps were bigger than my calves and his chest was so buff his T-shirt looked like it would burst. "My wife and I used a couple therapist."

My friend Craig, who'd joined the conversation, added a word of caution.

"I used a couple therapist too," he said. "They're only good for helping you break up." An imposing six-foot-four, Craig was even taller than Bill. He was a handsome television actor, also in his early sixties. His sad countenance seemed to confirm the weight of his words.

Bill was still with his wife and happily so, a fact he never tired of telling me. Craig had moved on from the woman he had been with. It was clear to me that Bill had found what he wanted in his therapy experience. Craig, too, even if it was not the answer he preferred.

The question was, would I?

Eight months earlier, in September 2014, I met a woman who threw me completely off balance, but the vertigo I experienced was a welcome gift. Her name was Zoe, and I fell in love with her more quickly than I imagined possible. She was fun, smart, sexy, a sometime actress, a college graduate with a science degree and a massage therapist. When I arrived at her studio for my first massage appointment, her smile, her laugh, her skilled hands, and a comfortable, genuine conversation all left me with a spreading electric charge in my muscles and a sense that I'd known her for years.

A week later, I asked her out. In a month, we were dating exclusively. Two months after that, we went away for a long weekend in San Diego, but in seven months we were breaking up and making up like teenagers. I should have seen the signs, but I didn't or wouldn't. I wanted the relationship to work. I wanted to marry Zoe.

Back at the gym, Craig read my mind.

"Go for it," he said. "A couple therapist might be right for you and Zoe."

"You think so?" I said, trying not to sound desperate.

"Absolutely," he said, then paused. "A therapist will help you see if she's the best partner for you. You ready for that?"

The music blared. The weights clanked. The guys around us grunted.

"Hmm," was all I could muster as I fidgeted with the small towel I always carried around during my morning workouts. If only I could use it to wipe away my anxiety about my tottering relationship.

Craig cocked his head and smiled down at me. "Let me know what you decide," he said, and we parted to finish our routines.

A few weeks later, on June 3, Zoe and I showed up at the office of a couple therapist not far from Zoe's apartment in Beverly Hills Adjacent. She dressed as if we were going on a date, including leopard-print four-inch heels, and I wore jeans and a T-shirt. Barely ten minutes into our first fifty-minute session, Zoe opened the door and pushed me onto the path that led, two years later, to my birth mother.

"Tell her about your adoption," she urged, turning to me as we sat, side by side, on the therapist's tan leather couch.

"My adoption?" I said, frowning, baffled at the idea. I stared hard at Zoe, then back at the therapist. "What does my adoption have to do with any of *this*?"

## 2

Zoe was thirty-five, I was fifty-seven.

Zoe took me on the first steps toward discovering my birth mother and seeing myself differently. Beautiful Zoe, whose brown gazelle eyes I craved looking into, who held my right hand in both her hands and massaged my palm when we drove around Los Angeles, who made it easy for me to trade in my car because it had a manual transmission and lease a new one with an automatic, so her hands weren't in competition with the four-on-the-floor. Zoe changed me in ways I was slow to realize.

She told me weeks after we met that our age difference never gave her a second thought. From our first date, we lost ourselves in lively, laughing conversation. Our first lunch at the now-closed Larchmont Bungalow lasted three hours.

Zoe was not put off when I told her that I identify as bisexual. She was filled with questions, and I expected that.

"It was hard to ask a woman out," I confessed to her.

"But you had no trouble asking guys, right?" she said.

"No," I said sheepishly, "but then I never *dated* guys."

She laughed a little and I realized she understood what I meant: like many of my gay friends, I preferred to skip the date and head directly to the bedroom, and every guy I hit on shared my enthusiasm. There are plenty of straight men and women who do the same thing, but Zoe made it clear that her values and upbringing did not make her one of them. Our emerging romance moved at her pace, not mine, and I was content. Relationships never blossomed with the few women I had dated before Zoe, and I hadn't slept with a guy in more than five years when Zoe came into my life.

She was a professional bodyworker, with skilled and intuitive hands and a technique that found every knot in my shoulders and back. She laughed at my silly jokes. Her skin was a deep black-brown and she wore her hair in a tight, natural curl, tinged cinnamon-bronze on its edges. It framed her head like a rusty dark halo, and I was smitten.

Zoe's smile was wide and revealed a small gap between her two front teeth. Her laugh was brassy. She liked to laugh, and I liked to hear her laugh. A second massage appointment followed on Sunday, September 14. As I dressed afterward, she pulled the linens from her table. She moved across the room with the grace of water, and I smiled to myself at the sight of her and the words slipped out of my mouth.

"Will you go out with me?" I asked.

She said yes. A happy accident because I was not looking to meet a woman. In fact, was not looking to meet anyone. We were different, yet not too different, and I had never been so happy as I was over the next fourteen months.

Zoe was born in Nigeria, nine degrees of latitude north of the equator. She moved with her family to Detroit when she was four, and helped her parents raise five younger siblings. She moved to Los Angeles in 2003, in her midtwenties.

Zoe was hot. Literally. Her body generated heat as if she had a built-in thermostat dial she could not turn down. She loved to spoon, but spooning became physically uncomfortable in a matter of minutes. I'd break out in a sweat and have to pull away, as if spooning were an omen, the first sign of trouble I did not see.

Our splitting up had nothing to do with age difference or race or my sexuality. The problem, if I could sum it up in a single word, was temperament. Ours did not mesh. We were engaged, unofficially, and I tried to hold on to this relationship to the furthest edge of its finality. I clung to it with my fingernails, right up to the moment when I had to say, "I'm done."

In resignation, I spoke those two words out loud, barely above a whisper. On the eve of my fifty-eighth birthday, in November 2015, while I sat on the bed Zoe and I shared, in the apartment we had rented together only three weeks earlier. *Three weeks.* Why didn't I see the signs? I did see the signs. But I did not pay attention to them. I moved to the sofa in the living room. Two months later, I moved out.

Years later, I realized that Zoe knew something about adoption that I did not know she knew. She knew something about adoption that I did not know. She never said anything to me about what she may have known, and I could be wrong—it is only a feeling I have in my gut. But why would she have asked me to talk about my adoption with the therapist if she did not have some idea that it was relevant? Everyone seemed to know so much about adoption that I did not know.

As easy as conversation was between Zoe and me, a clue that something was not right between us emerged only later, something I wish I had been mindful of in the moment: we knew how to have great talks, but I see now that we did not know how to communicate with one another. Zoe and I never talked about my adoption. She had no idea what it meant when she spoke up at our first couple therapy session, or where it would lead, except that she must have had some prior knowledge about adoption that she never shared with me.

Zoe would be as much a catalyst in my journey as George Watson was. It was Zoe who led me in 2015 to the therapist who introduced me to the author of two books that would change my life: Nancy Newton Verrier, M.A., a psychotherapist in private practice and an adoption specialist. Two people—my couple therapist and Verrier—marked the beginning of my education about what I think most people would agree was a consequential event in my life, but one that I never gave much thought to. Everything I knew about adoption would be challenged.

Verrier's books, *The Primal Wound: Understanding the Adopted Child* and *Coming Home To Self: The Adopted Child Grows Up*, are considered primers among many adoptees and adoption specialists. But her thinking unnerved me. Speaking to me not as if from the pages of a book but as if we sat across from one another in a private therapy session, Verrier said that I had suffered a deep wound and that if I argued with her about this interpretation, I was in denial of my suffering.

As she wrote in *The Primal Wound* in describing infants, "It is thought by many psychologists that [...] a feeling of rightness, well-being and wholeness [...] is a state of primary narcissism considered appropriate to this stage of life." But when the infant is separated from their birth mother, the "opposites of this state are the feelings of anxiety, sorrow, and loneliness."

Then I felt a punch to my gut:

Speaking in reference to anxiety, sorrow, and loneliness, she wrote, "These are the feelings most often described by those adoptees who have at last ceased to deny or repress their feelings."

And then one more punch:

"The search for Self is a mission for many adoptees who believe that their 'baby soul' was annihilated upon the separation from the original mother." She is unclear about her meaning of "baby soul" so I am left to guess that it refers to an adoptee's essence, a deep part of themselves.

As I read Verrier, she seemed to give no quarter to nuance or personal experience. Her promise of clarity and insight came at a steep price.

An interior war with Verrier broke out within me almost as soon as I began reading her books, and I argued with her in my head. Instead of playing the teacher and the guide, which I sought and expected, she emerged as an unwelcome heckler whom I could not silence. Respected, yes, but she and her theories were uninvited. She planted six venomous words in my head that would haunt me for years: *you were the victim of trauma*.

## 3

Never has a fifty-minute therapy session walloped me like my first one with Zoe, and I've been in therapy before. The idea was to salvage our relationship, yet I left reeling, second-guessing my entire childhood. A childhood I had thought was happy—idyllic, in fact.

When I arrived at the therapist's office, I expected to face hard work, more than a little anguish, painful self-exploration, and to acquire the tools we needed to begin repairing our broken relationship. I never imagined I'd leave there questioning something as settled as my origin story. The task I faced now doubled in degree of difficulty. There were not one but two off-kilter relationships: my romance with Zoe and the esteem I had for myself, for the image reflected at me every day in the mirror. These I had not bargained for.

Our therapist laid out a process and I was prepared to submit myself completely to it. To make amends, examine myself as closely as I could, compromise where it was called for, stand fast when necessary. These steps I was ready for.

But I felt ambushed by the supposition that my adoption played a role in my relationship with Zoe. I knew nothing about adoption research, and I had never heard of Nancy Verrier. When

Zoe asked me to talk about my adoption in this setting, I was incredulous. Her request felt irrelevant, untethered.

I did the only thing I knew how to do: I compartmentalized. The Zoe problem dropped into a box over *here*, the self-esteem problem into a box over *there*. I would work on the contents of one box at a time because I was a miserable multitasker. Never mind that most humans these days are multitaskers. No one else had my conundrums.

My therapist's suggestion to read Nancy Verrier's books was not an edict, and I could have ignored her. I didn't. Still, her books were not easy reads, her pronouncements were like fingernails on a blackboard. My inclination was to push back against her arguments, but that meant I had to read them and understand them.

In those days I had only my lived experience and gut instincts as my defense. Years would pass before I discovered an ally of equal stature to Verrier. Beginning in the fall of 2015 and lasting into early 2017, I plodded through her two volumes, each cataloging her long list of adoptee character flaws, her case studies, her dark explanations of trauma that she claimed arose from adoption.

When I protested about Verrier to my therapist, she pushed back herself with the same certainty as Verrier. Cracks emerged in my facade even as I held my ground. Was it possible that Verrier could be right?

My sister Linda, the youngest biological child of my mom and dad, became my ally. More than anyone else in my family Linda has been my constant companion on the journey of understanding the new, confusing twists of being an adoptee. She's a lawyer and she brought an ordered thinking to my outlook, which I admit was sometimes overwrought.

Linda was a sympathetic listener, but sometimes she surprised me with revelations about my childhood. There was something unflappable about my little sister. She wore her Catholic faith—she had converted from our family's Congregational upbringing when she married my brother-in-law Mike—like armor, and with a positive note that made me feel more confident in my own beliefs. Late in my life I discovered that she and I shared similar views on God and spirituality and our conversations about my adoption often included her insights on her beliefs. I fed off her and I would like to think she felt the same way.

When we were little, Linda was in the unique position as an observer. She remembered events that never imprinted on my memory but somehow remained fresh in hers, and one day she stunned me with a recollection about my past. We were on the phone, and she said, "You didn't like Mom's cooking. I was frozen in my seat one night at dinner when you lost it."

I was a picky eater when I was young. Mom was no chef, but she always served fresh everything: meats, vegetables, fruits, milk, orange juice.

"You stood up (from the dining table) screaming," Linda said, her tone disbelieving even after fifty years, "and said 'I hate this! I hate this! I hate this!' And then you stormed out of the house, jumped on your bike, and rode off. Mom and Dad sat in silence. I didn't know what to do, so I sat there, too. No one said anything for a long time."

As she spoke, I could tell—even over the telephone—she wanted to laugh and cringe at the same moment. I had no doubt she was telling me the truth, but I wished she had been making it up. As she recalled it, I rode my bike—I must have been eleven or twelve—to the Lake Shore Swim and Tennis Club, where we were members, about a mile away from our house in the northern suburbs of Milwaukee and ordered my favorites from the grill: a cheeseburger and fries and charged it to the family account.

There is no doubt that Linda's memory was accurate and that I was guilty of an embarrassing display of rudeness and entitlement. And I remembered none of it.

Linda surprised me further when she said this was not an isolated incident.

"You did this many times," she recalled. "Until it snowed or rained, and you couldn't ride your bike to the club."

"What did Mom and Dad do?" I asked.

"Nothing. They never stopped you."

An amateur psychologist could see I was testing boundaries. Well, *testing* may have been an understatement.

Even in Linda's most diplomatic retelling of this story, my interpretation of this personal episode seemed to confirm at least some of Verrier's unflattering notions about adoptees.

Was my behavior at the family dinner table an example of the psychic scaring Verrier diagnosed in adoptees? Was I blind to this fact? Was Linda's recollection proof of Verrier's claim that I was a victim of trauma?

"You were a kid acting like a kid," said Noel, a friend, who laughed out loud when I retold my dinner-table story. He knew about my adoption. He knew I had been struggling with Verrier's books. Noel was a retired Air Force colonel, a decorated combat vet who'd served in the first Iraqi war. "I wouldn't overthink it."

Noel was also the father of two boys, now in their midtwenties. Because I never had children I had no frame of reference.

"I could tell you some stories," he said, shaking his head on one of our regular FaceTime calls, a wry smile on his tanned, round face. He wore his hair short, a military cut. "Both my boys could tell you stories, too."

My buddy did not reveal specifics about his boys' misdeeds growing up, but he spoke with such calm authority that his reassurances made me feel a little better. Still, I had some doubts. Verrier had gotten under my skin.

# 4

Verrier got under my skin because I allowed her to get under my skin. But I was also consumed by a long grieving for the end of my relationship with Zoe and my head was clouded. My gym buddy Craig proved to be right when he'd told me couple therapy's only benefit was to end a disintegrating relationship.

I continued working with the therapist because I needed to talk about my failed relationship, but also because I was fascinated by my therapist's insights about adoption, even though the more I read Verrier, the more I disagreed with my therapist about her.

Thankfully, my therapist was more interested in me than in Verrier and she became my sounding board as I waded through the books and began the slow crawl through the muck of a love that did not last. I remembered a line from a poet who wrote that loving is brief and forgetting seems endless. I hoped he was wrong, but I was doubting it in those early days of my mourning.

Recovery and letting go marked 2016: a recovery of my equilibrium, thrown off by Verrier, and a letting go of lost love. Every friend who had an opinion about getting over a relationship told me the grief period lasts about as long as the relationship itself, so I steeled myself for fifteen months of returning from the land of the dead. My friends exaggerated, but not by much. The year felt like a slow-motion slinking through sobbing everywhere: in my shower, standing at the kitchen sink, sitting at my computer, or folding my laundry. Then I experienced a manic, polar opposite, and I concocted fantasies of starting over with Zoe. I was darn close to donning the garb of torch bearer. My Jersey Kitty is a Calico, a breed of feline known for its gregarious, affectionate nature, but I could have used an obsequious support animal for cuddling and comfort. Richard Simmons came to mind.

At the same time, like a new driver with one foot on the gas pedal and the other on the brake, I lurched my way through Nancy Verrier's books. One moment I was clear-headed enough to be fascinated by her observations and conclusions even when I found them objectionable, the next I was the adoptee unrepresented in her supposedly scholarly work, raising my voice in my empty apartment and talking back to printed words on a page. And sometimes I flung her books across the room like a baseball pitcher aiming for the head of the batter. One or the other would smack the wall and land flat on the floor, spine cracked, a few pages bent and dirtied. I would smolder at it in contempt, arms and legs and eyebrows crossed. Jersey would perk up at the rude sound of the book, then return to her slumber on the couch next to me. I wish I had been more like her. Someone said that when you're going through hell, keep going. So, I lurched and crawled and flung, lurched, and crawled and flung.

Why on earth did I imagine that reading someone as depressing as Nancy Verrier would be a distraction to a relationship breakup? It baffles me now, but that was my course of action. Reading two textbooks on adoption research was not high on my list of things to do. It was not even on my list. I love to read, but this was homework and it felt like homework. So why did I read two books? Well...these books were about me, about adoptees, and I wanted to learn more about me.

But with a title like *The Primal Wound*, the prospects were intimidating. Think about it: You're adopted, you've always known you were adopted, it was never a secret growing up, and you've never had any problem with the notion of being adopted. No issues. Not one. Not ever.

Then in your late fifties, your couple therapist tells you a lot has been uncovered in only the last twenty years and you know nothing about it. Oh, and by the way: The book she wanted me to read tells me I'm wounded. Whether I know it or not.

Nancy Verrier spared me nothing, and on page one I confronted the dilemma. She claims that the accepted wisdom of the bonding process doesn't begin at birth but is a "continuum" of events that are physical, psychological, and spiritual. They begin in utero, she says, and move through postnatal bonding. But when the newborn is separated from the mother after birth, the damage, including abandonment and loss, is permanent. Verrier called this the Primal Wound.

But by page two, I also saw, though it didn't fully register, the first flaw in her thinking:

"And yet, how can one prove or even support something which is preverbal, such as a wound to the psyche resulting from a trauma about which a person has no conscious memory? As a clinician, I can only infer such feelings and experiences with the help of those adoptees who allow themselves to go that far back into their pain. As a biological mother, I can know it through my own intuition and experience, a knowing which is not always observable by anyone else. At the current state of our understanding, such inferences can neither be proved nor disproved, only believed or disbelieved."

I could have stopped right there, put down the book and been done with the whole business. In a few paragraphs, Verrier admitted that her evidence was only clinical, based solely on self-selected adoptees who came to her for help, not a random, double-blind study with a control group that typically defines scientific research. She did not talk to adoptees like me because adoptees like me felt no need to talk to her. And she was relying at least in part on her experience as a mother.

But I kept reading because my therapist urged me to continue, and because I like to finish what I start. On page nineteen Verrier wrote that it is not possible to break the connection with the biological mother and replace it with another primary caregiver "no matter how warm, caring, and motivated she may be" without serious consequences for both the child and the mother. "Bonding may be difficult, or as many adoptees told me, impossible," she added.

In other words, I thought, she seemed to say *screw Mom*. No matter what she did, according to Verrier, Mom was a poor substitute for my birth mother. Worse, she was no substitute at all. Mom's love for me would not measure up and left me scarred or rather "wounded" to use Verrier's terminology.

I felt cold and incredulous. I searched my memory, I plumbed my heart, and I could not find any experience, any anecdote, nothing, that resembled even a hint of the picture Verrier was trying to draw of the woman who raised me.

She comes to the thesis of her book on page twenty-one, and the emphasis is hers:

"It is my belief, therefore, that *the severing of that connection between the adopted child and his birthmother causes a primal or narcissistic wound, which affects the adoptee's sense of Self and often manifests in a sense of loss, basic mistrust, anxiety and depression, emotional and/or behavioral problems, and difficulties in relationships with significant others.*"

I wondered if I would have felt more offended had I been accused of a felony without recourse to defend myself. I seethed. I bristled. The book was lucky to have been only flung against my wall.

By pages 181–82, I came to her most definitive statements:

"Babies should never be separated from their mothers unless it is absolutely necessary," she wrote, "because separation causes trauma, and trauma leaves the child wounded. The wound affects adoptees all their lives and greatly impacts their relationships with others as they go through the life cycle [...] Yet one of the residues of abandonment is a perpetual feeling of being a victim, of being powerless, of being helpless to help oneself."

There it was: adoptees are victims of The Primal Wound. I admit I'm a layperson, but her statements did not leave room for discussion.

In her second book, *Coming Home to Self*, she cataloged adoption issues and turned them into sharp elbows to the gut. Here's a summary of a few chapter headings for only Part 1: separation trauma; hyper-arousal; anxiety; terror; hyper vigilance; repetition compulsion; dissociation, numbing or constriction; disconnection; not belonging; blaming the victim; fear; fear of being disliked; fear of inner states of mind; anger and rage; sorrow: the ubiquitous emotion; joy: the elusive emotion...

That's a sampling and it covers only the first 125 pages of a 480-page text.

If any one person displayed even a handful of these personality—what's the right word?—challenges? Abnormalities? Quirks? My goodness, their head would explode.

As I read through the compendium of personal malfunctions, I wondered if my entire personality were suddenly reduced to read like an FDA-mandated list of drug side effects one finds stuffed inside a new bottle of aspirin.

And that's when it hit me. She wasn't describing *me* or any *single* adoptee. She was compiling a *laundry list* of all the behaviors she'd uncovered in the adoptees she has studied or interviewed.

In other words, the adoptees in pain who sought her out for help.

When I took a deep breath and understood Verrier's broader purpose, giving me a new lens to view her collection of adoptee acting-out symptoms, I still did not recognize myself in the picture she drew. Here and there I saw things that were familiar—a short fuse, hypersensitivity to criticism, scant tolerance for frustration—but was that enough to lump me in with her sweeping diagnosis she called the Primal Wound?

Plenty of people who are *not* adopted have quick tempers and thin skins. Some have become president of the United States. And psychologists.

But was I really a victim of trauma the way she defined it? The nuts-and-bolts details in Verrier's books seemed incongruous at best, wildly fantastical at worst, from anything I had experienced in my life. I could not give her credence. Or if I gave her credit for some of her observations about adoptees, anyone with half a brain could ask reasonably, "Are you saying only adoptees display these symptoms?"

Trauma as a broad concept made sense—of course a child taken from its mother at birth will suffer some kind of wound—but Verrier was describing pathologies, not people, and even a layperson could see this. Moreover, her evidence, as I read it, was based on feelings—her own as a mother and those she cataloged from the adoptees she interviewed who were troubled by their adoptions. Where was the comparative control group?

In spite of my critique of Verrier's theories and her work, somehow her voice had moved into my brain, and I struggled to shut it up. Worse, I knew I had both the tools and the personal experience to parry her arguments. But instead of letting it go and moving on, I stewed.

## 5

Spurred by a frustration with Verrier that drove me to find some alternative theory or a counter-factual to her Primal Wound, I stumbled across an online forum on the website adoption.com discussing a topic that sounded more like science fiction than science: the Ghost Kingdom. The moderator of this chat excerpted a passage from the author and adoption counselor, Betty F. Lifton, who described this realm:

"In my book *Journey of the Adopted Self* (Lifton, 1994), I introduced the Ghost Kingdom, where the adopted child keeps the lost birth mother, birth father, and his original self, the eternal ghost baby who was not able to grow up. The Ghost Kingdom is an alternate place, located in one's psychic reality. It is a portable Home that adoptees carry inside them. It is the Land of What Might Have Been. It is the Land of the As If Dead."

I remember staring blankly at these words, then crunching my eyebrows together in confusion, as if I'd turned on a radio and every station was broadcast in a foreign language. The author and everyone in this chat were serious, and I had to stifle my laughter. The Ghost Kingdom was more than a metaphor. For them it was real.

Everyone on this forum seemed to be comfortable underwater, and I was flopping around on land, out of my depth. Ghost baby? Alternate place? The land of what might have been? Who were these people?

But I credit Lifton, whose idea sparked the online conversation I found, with solidifying the correctness of my lived experience. Because buried within a long string of comments about Ghost Kingdom was this line:

"...so let's try not to turn this into the same old kicking of the dead horse; well adjusted, happy, good adoptees vs. maladjusted, angry, bad adoptee debate, if we can help it. lol"

Happy, good adoptees versus maladjusted, angry, bad adoptees?

Polarization within the adoptee community itself? The comment suggested previous and perhaps long-running disagreements between the two sides. It was a surprising, and to be honest, a welcome revelation despite the snarky name-calling.

Without ever realizing it or having made any conscious choice, I knew where I stood: firmly in the "happy, good adoptee" camp. As far as I was concerned, I didn't need to join the debate.

# 6

---

Everything I knew, and had ever known, about my birth mother and birth father fit on a five-by-seven-inch sheet of white notepaper in my Dad's compact, annoyingly neat, slanted handwriting. As a physician, he would have been a dream for any pharmacist who puzzled over a doctor's illegible prescription. But Dad was a radiologist, who read X-rays and made diagnoses from them. He was licensed to write prescriptions, but he never did so far as I know.

His note was folded twice and placed in a three-by-five white envelope, with no date. I don't remember when I first saw it, but I do know it was sometime in the late 1980s.

Dad gave me what amounted to a treasure trove tucked inside an ordinary envelope. Only the writing on the envelope was remarkable. A flourish I had never seen from my dad: a blue-ink swirl beneath my name. He must have been in an especially cheerful mood.

The note read:

Howard

Mother

5' 3" Greek + German-English

Dark blue eyes
Light brown hair
Medium complexion – av. Weight 120#
Graduate Nurse
Very attractive woman
Good in portrait painting, arts & crafts
Siblings – tall, intelligent & interested in art
Lawyer
FBI
Engineer
Valedictorian
Father
5' 8" Scots-Irish
Dark brown eyes & hair
High school grad + 2 yr. college
Husky build
Very musically inclined
Can play any instrument

FOR DECADES, for as long as I had been alive, I was content to know this scant bit of information. To know *only* this. What more did I need? More importantly, why would I need it?

Today, decades after Dad gave me this note, as someone comfortable with introspection, about learning more about myself, my answers are the same: I had all that I needed. What Dad gave me was enough. What Mom and Dad gave me as my adoptive parents more than made up for what my birth mother and birth father chose not to give me.

After Dad handed me the envelope and I read it, I placed it in a pale blue plastic storage container I'd purchased to hold all the letters I have kept from family and friends. Only once have I pulled it out—to research this chapter. My curiosity about my adoption stopped there and remained sealed, like the pale blue storage container tucked away in my cabinet.

If I had chosen to undergo a search for my birth mother years ago, I would have faced a long series of obstacles, a prolonged hunt, considerable expenses, and long waits. This was the reality for adoptees in "closed adoption" states such as Wisconsin. The law was explicit and favored the birth mother's privacy. I could have hired a private investigator to do the work, but I lacked the one element necessary to start: the desire. I had none. Why, I thought then, would I torture myself with these trials?

There was no existential angst welling up in me, no profound longing to fill in blanks in my past. From my perspective, I was a happy, pampered, privileged child who wanted for virtually nothing, who had been adopted into an upper-middle-class home, with an extended family that sprawled across much of the Midwest, beginning with Mom and Dad and then me, followed by Mary Jo, then Mike, and finally Linda. Our home base was on Jonathan Lane in a neighborhood called Orchard Highlands in a village called Bayside on the northern edge of Milwaukee County.

Mary Jo is a beautiful name and Mom chose it to mimic her name, Martha Joyce, but I preferred to call her Jo and she did not object. Like me, Jo had also been adopted, but from a different birth mother. She joined Mom, Dad, and me in 1958, two years after I arrived. Mike was born in 1961, and Linda in 1962, three and four years later respectively. They were Mom and Dad's biological children. Two adoptees, two biologicals. We were a modern family. There's an old wives' tale that says when couples struggle to conceive and then they adopt, this somehow releases whatever had been bottled up and the biological babies arrive. The problem is, there is scant evidence to back this up. But the myth persists.

Jo was a natural athlete with a shock of white-blond hair when she was young who gravitated to swimming and later, in high school, she became an equestrian. She earned a master's degree in education and taught elementary school for twenty-five years.

But it was Jo who reminded me years later that she and I

sometimes spoke in a private vocabulary when we were growing up. I'd completely forgotten about this. When we talked about our *biological moms* and *biological dads*, no one else in our circle used such words. Those were the accepted terms of our day. They are acceptable today as well, but not preferred, such as birth mother or birth father. The phrase "politically correct" had not yet entered the lexicon, much less my consciousness.

Mike was also drawn to sports and loved basketball and every Wisconsin sports team, college and professional alike. But he had problems at birth, and Mom and Dad did not comprehend what had happened until he was two or three. Our pediatrician suspected that Mike was deprived of oxygen during Mom's labor, and the result was what we called mental retardation back then, but today we would refer to as a cognitive disability. He attended special education classes until his accidental drowning just before his nineteenth birthday. Linda, the baby of the family, almost six years my junior, was always a mystery to me if only because she was so much younger, but she shared Jo's love of horses and I was awed and impressed by both of their horseback-riding skills. They amassed an enviable collection of ribbons and trophies, and more than a few dramatic photographs capturing them in mid-air, which covered the walls of the family room in our house on Jonathan Lane. Linda served as an assistant attorney general in Texas and is the senior legal counsel for the University of Texas system in Austin.

Then there was Mom's parents, my favorite grandparents. Grandpa Mendenhall and Grandma, whom we called Gogan, a made-up name with a long family history. Gogan was a writer and a window dresser for Marshall Field's, a well-known department store, and I like to think the grandparent who was my most ardent champion creatively and influenced me the most. Grandpa was an electrical engineer. They lived about half an hour away on a lily-padded, spring-fed lake populated with families, and surrounded by farmland, an ideal escape especially in the summer.

Grandma and Grandpa Ibach, Dad's parents, lived ninety minutes west in Madison, the capitol of Wisconsin. Dad's brother, my Uncle Paul and his family lived a couple hours south and a bit west in northern Illinois. Farther to the west, more relations lived on or near the Mississippi River, and then deeper into Minnesota, more cousins, aunts, and uncles on both sides of the family. Our roots in these Midwest states dug deeply.

My memory of Julys as a family reunion month is pungent as fresh-mown grass. We would pile into the station wagon and motor west as the song tells us, sometimes southwest, usually within Wisconsin, often into Illinois and Minnesota, occasionally all the way to Iowa, because we didn't have to go farther. We had more welcoming stopping points, with faces familiar and smiling and sunburnt, family members standing on front porches, in driveways, kneeling in gardens, arms outstretched in open-mouthed surprise to see us pull up, than we could ever visit in a single summer.

Mom and Dad—Harold and Martha—followed the advice of the 1950s for new adoptive parents. Whenever you speak to your son—this is what they told me they were told—always say some version of, "How are you adopted son?" or "Good morning, adopted son." The phrase "adopted son" was tacked onto any statement or question directed at me. The phrasing sounded awkward and still does. Mom and Dad no doubt found it awkward, too. As the infant who became a toddler on the receiving end of these statements, however, I evidently found these words, well, everyday Mom- and Dad-talk. Nothing more.

"What does 'adopted' mean?" I asked one day. I was three, maybe four years old.

Mom and Dad looked at each other in frozen silence, trying to figure out who would answer and what they would say.

"When you were born," Mom said, "your mother couldn't keep you for herself, so we picked you. We chose you as our son."

This tale—"We picked you. You were chosen"—remained

with me unquestioned, as a child, a youth, as an adult. In fact, I liked it. These six words made me feel content. Somewhere I read an article about a young woman who was the last child in her family. She had been told by her parents that she was a "mistake." She had not been intended.

How could a parent admit to any child of theirs that they were a mistake, much less speak those words out loud to an offspring? It provoked a thought: was I a mistake? The question crept into my thinking, but I answered emphatically by reaffirming the cherished story Mom and Dad had given me—I was picked out. It provided a solid floor to stand on.

And something else that I did not comprehend until decades later: This story, no matter how fairy-tale-like it sounded, was the first building block from Mom and Dad that allowed me to begin writing my own narrative. "You were picked out" was an explanation meant for a child, but I grabbed it, made it mine, and constructed a biography.

As a kid, I envisioned, in a dream or waking idyll, a long line of baby cribs lined up in what I imagined to be the "special adoption place," and Mom and Dad strolling slowly from one crib to the next. And then they reached my crib.

"He's the one!" Mom said.

"You bet," said Dad.

"Let's take him home," she said.

This is how we talk in Wisconsin.

How could I think anything negatively about being adopted? Why would I have cared about some anonymous woman who did not want to raise me herself? More to the point, I did not care. She made me available for adoption all those years ago. Her loss, my gain.

My boyhood friends were curious, however, especially if I was the first adoptee they had met. They asked what it meant to be adopted, and I gave my answer, which became a memorized speech.

"When I was born," I would say, "my biological mom couldn't keep me. I don't know why. Nobody knows why. She just had to give me away. So, I was adopted when I was a few weeks old."

It was a little boy's answer. My words were sincere, but rote. I knew the meaning of the words I uttered, but I did not understand their implication, nor did I comprehend their weight. The choice of the words I used, "give me away," along with others I may have said and have certainly learned about over the years, is peculiar. These utterances crackle, as if they would shock like static electricity. When you hear "I was turned over to" or "I was given up for adoption" or "I was surrendered for adoption," they hint of a physical struggle, like a melee that ended in a shiner and a bloodied lip.

Yet, if, as a child, I spoke these words or heard them spoken to me or about me, they registered with no more impact than a whisper.

My friends may have asked another question or two about my adoption. Most did not. They simply nodded and accepted my answer. But I kept telling this story well into adulthood. Sincere, but rote.

Only once can I recall that my adoption emerged as a potential roadblock. As a sophomore at Nicolet High School in Milwaukee I had earned a spot on the junior varsity basketball team. I loved the game and was dedicated to it since I was a starter on my seventh- and eighth-grade teams at Maple Dale elementary school. I made the freshman team as well at Nicolet, but I worked harder than I expected to make JV and I was not a starter. Of course, I said I wanted to make the varsity squad, but I spoke the words with no real conviction.

One day at JV practice, the coach told us to stand in a single-file line and one by one, he asked each of us a question. Waiting somewhere in the middle of the line, I did not hear him at first.

Then he stepped in front of me.

"How tall is your father?" he asked.

As a sophomore, I stood five-eight. In seventh and eighth grade, I was among the tallest in my class, and for both grades I played the position of first-string center, a skinny chimp-like kid with long arms and big hands. I had radar focus at swatting away others' shots and only mediocre accuracy at making my own. On the high school JV team, I was no longer the tallest among my classmates. My body had caught up with my appendages and I was now playing second-string forward.

"He's five-six," I said and instantly added, "but I was adopted. His height won't have anything to do with my height." I was sincere, but rote.

At first my coach said nothing. He did not move and only stared at me. Then I saw his face change. His eyebrows constricted, his mouth turned down in a slight frown.

"I don't believe you," he said. He was not angry or gruff. He was as matter of fact with me as I had been with him. I opened my mouth to object, but I was cut off by my friends.

"Yeah, he was adopted."

"He's telling the truth."

"He's right. He was adopted."

The voices came from the friends who knew me the longest, who had known me since kindergarten. They spoke almost in unison like a friendly Greek chorus. They came to my defense. They protested on my behalf before I could say a thing.

My coach was after a basic insight, a clue about how much taller each of us might become. How tall our dads were was the evidence he sought. My coach must have assumed I knew why he was asking and that I made up an adoption story to throw him off. He was recruiting for the varsity coach, but I did not know this at the time. He backed down after hearing my friends' objections and claimed to accept my story. Looking back on these events almost five decades later, I see the simple gesture of friendship these boys offered. They had my back. At the time, all I cared about was playing basketball.

My adoption never spurred much curiosity in me, but I was in most other ways a curious child. I grew up with my own origin story. Children who are not adopted, who are the biological offspring of their parents, usually ask some version of "Where did I come from?" as they grow up. I may have asked that question, too, but I have no recollection.

# 7
---

My wish is to go back to the 1960s and be inside my head, if only for a few moments. Even though the experience would be excruciating for any adult, I imagine a make-believe exchange between my ten-year-old self and Nancy Verrier. Ridiculous, I know, but bear with me.

"You were abandoned!" she would say to me. "By your own mother! Doesn't that make you feel terrible?"

*Abandoned, shabandoned. Mom and Dad are taking us to Disneyland for Christmas!*

"She rejected you! Doesn't that hurt?"

*We're flying on a real airplane! I've never been on one of those before.*

"You suffered a psychic wound!" her voice would hiss. "Aren't you sad?"

*Next year we're going to Acapulco. That's in Mexico! And what is a sick-o wound anyway?*

My memory strains trying to imagine myself as a child addressing these adult questions. They were preposterous. These overblown and abstract notions meant nothing to a kid in the Ibach household who was having as much fun as I was.

In 2016 and into 2017, as I finished reading Nancy Verrier's books about the Primal Wound, I knew her theory had thrown me off balance. She taunted me about being the victim of trauma. I started to doubt my own story. I wondered if she knew me better than I knew myself.

But then I found the antidote: my childhood and my memories of it. Replaying those memories rebalanced my equilibrium. The indelible film loops I watched in my head erased the doubts I had about who I was and where I belonged. Remembering helped me remember.

## 8

---

I grew up in Wisconsin, where snow is a fact of life. Snow scrunching is the ubiquitous sound car tires make many months of the year. The sound brings me back to perhaps the most enduring memory of my life in the early 1960s and of the life Mom, a scientist, and Dad, a World War II vet and later a physician, gave me and my siblings. The memory may be the happiest of all my childhood recollections and I have many.

It began with the family station wagon scrunching its way through fresh snow on the narrow streets of Orchard Highlands, our neighborhood, heard above the non-stop chatter of my brother and sisters in the back seat, over the intense blowing of the car heater. The noisy tires slowed, then came to a stop, the last sound like cracking wood.

Why was Dad stopping at the entrance of our driveway? My siblings and I fell silent in unison. We stared out the car windows. We were returning home from Christmas Eve services at North Shore Congregational Church a few miles away.

"Who turned the lights on?" said my sister, Jo. The rule at our house on Jonathan Lane was inviolate: leave the house, turn out the lights. This was 1963, long before "energy crisis" became part of anyone's vocabulary a decade later. This was Mom's influence.

I was seven. Jo, five. Mike was two and a half, and Linda eighteen months.

To silence the lot of us all at once took much more than "Don't make me pull this car over" from Mom or Dad.

It wasn't only the porch lights, but all the interior lights blazing in the house. All of them: the front hall, the living room just beyond, the laundry room and bathroom and the kitchen to the left of the front door, and all the bathroom windows facing the driveway to the right. Every light in our house had been turned on and all the exterior lights as well. The Christmas lights strung on the tree in our front yard glowed red and green. The place was a beacon. A colorful holiday beacon.

Dad didn't say a word, nor did Mom, as if they had expected to see the house lit up. But I didn't think about that until many years later. In the moment, I was captured by the unfolding drama. Dad let his foot off the brake and the tires scrunched their way through the compacted snow into our driveway until we stopped at the curb of the concrete patio leading to our front door.

Someone squealed. Probably Jo. It could have been me.

But I'll never forget what we saw through the two vertical panes of glass in the double front doors.

Santa Claus!

The sedate family station wagon exploded in high-pitched ecstatic screams, like caged birds, as if my sisters, brother, and I had been plugged into an active electric outlet. I can only imagine how Mom and Dad reacted, Mom who spoke with deliberateness to avoid offending, and Dad who rarely spoke at all. We may have scared them half to death in our excitement.

I know we scared the pants off Santa. He had been doing what Santa was supposed to do: delivering presents and arranging them beneath the tree, which was clearly visible from our vantage in the driveway through the front doors.

Except that our sudden appearance, accompanied by a crescendo of childish exuberance, roused Santa from his elfish revelry. He glanced out the front door windows at us. We were staring at him. And then he exited stage left. We knew what was there: a sliding-glass door off the dining room on the backside of the house. Beyond that was nothing but snow-covered yard and beyond that a wooded ravine.

For a fraction of a second, all of us—me, Jo, Mike, and Linda —were too stunned to move. But only for a fraction of a second. The eruption inside the car spilled out the door and we scrambled into the house and to the threshold of the now-open sliding-glass door.

All we found were deep boot tracks in the snow stepping off into the darkened backyard.

But it did not matter. We had seen what, or rather who, we had all hoped we would see, and were shocked into childish exuberance because we had interrupted him in the middle of his yuletide business.

We saw Santa Claus.

In the flesh. In his red suit and stocking hat, black belt and shiny buckle, black boots, and, of course, his long white beard. It was him, all right. No mistake.

Mom and Dad chose to remain quiet, on the sidelines, when the family station wagon came to a stop as we fixated on Santa just inside our front doors. Mom said nothing. Dad said nothing. They let the scene play out on its own. What could they have done to add to, much less top, the gift of magic unfolding before our eyes?

It took me a year or more to learn the truth, that the bearded, red-suited, jolly fellow in our house, framed by the bright white lights and Christmas glow wasn't really Santa Claus.

It was Mr. Mintz. Gerald Mintz, the father of school friends who lived a few houses down the road. I never found out who, between Mom and Dad, conjured up the idea. Each would have claimed the other as the author. But I am as certain as I can be, without actual proof, that Mom was the one to thank. I'm sure it was she who persuaded Gerald Mintz to play along, a role he told me many years later took no persuading. It was a cherished memory for him, too.

I have many memories of my childhood in our home in Bayside, a quiet, verdant, forested quadrant seemingly frozen in time. Mine was a Disney and Bob's Big Boy and John Glenn and Gunsmoke and Mickey Mouse childhood. And Mom was the architect. Smiles and laughter, summer camp and catching fireflies, and the occasional parental spanking for roughing up on one or both sisters who probably deserved it, but as I was reminded before the administration of a hand to my bottom, I was supposed to know better. Because I was the big brother.

What I do not remember are many warm words or hugs or much affection and the truth was, a lot of us growing up and living in the upper Midwest in this era probably recall the same thing. I was not unique.

That short Christmas scene summed up my childhood, or at least the best of it, enshrined in a loop of film I replay in my head, lasting no more than a few seconds. It comes back to me regardless of the season, but most often in December. Mr. Mintz did all the work. But Mom set the wheels in motion, and Dad played along.

Though my parents were, at best, adequate at the emotional stuff of child-rearing, I understood that Mom and Dad knew how to love. They loved us the best way they could and that was enough. The Christmas when Santa stopped by on his rounds was the single best "I love you" Mom and Dad ever did not say out loud.

## 9

I wonder if Mom and Dad had any idea that the house they built in 1958 would imprint so deeply on my being. They built this structure on a piece of land secluded on a cul-de-sac encircled by a ravine. I have a single tattoo on my upper left arm inked when I was thirty-eight, and it is a pale comparison to the permanent vividness of the images, the sounds, the smells, and the feel, even the taste, I can conjure at any moment of this parcel of land and the place I called home.

The structure was unique, and I never needed photographs to remember the rooms and their walls. My parents hired an architect who designed the home to their specifications. The dwelling seemed to emerge from its surroundings. I always saw it as something that belonged there, tucked within rather than imposed on its setting.

The first time I saw a satellite photograph of my neighborhood on Google Earth, I was stunned by the wing-like shape of our house when viewed from above. But the overhead image flattened its features, one of which was a soaring twin-peaked roof that connected the two "wings" of the house in the middle. Imagine an enormous bird whose head and tail paled compared to its massive wingspan. In front, the peak resembled a massive wood awning that covered a concrete patio over the front doors. On the backside of the house, the other even larger peak swept higher, reaching toward the treetops, yet it was almost unseen from the street side. I think this is an accurate reflection of Harold and Martha, who were not ostentatious.

The "curb appeal" of the house brings out an appreciative nod. But only when you are standing in the privacy of the back-yard do you feel a quick intake of breath. The roofline on this side floated over the tiered backyard. This peaked roof, immodest compared to the one in front, projected a bold statement, enclosed the living room with a vaulted ceiling that reached fifteen feet, and split floor-to-ceiling windows down the middle with an immense fireplace, made of fieldstone on the exterior. A soaring shiny copper hood, an immense enclosure that ran from the ceiling down to the opening of the fireplace, which was protected by a sliding metal curtain you could draw aside to add logs, dominated the living room. Attached to its base was a smooth marble seat that wrapped around the fireplace. The seat had openings on both sides with room beneath to store wood and tinder.

The entire home acted like an arrow pointing into the woods, as if to say to all visitors: explore. I remember feeling like Captain Nemo, but instead of being aboard the Nautilus and peering out a porthole at the underwater scenery, I perched at the living-room windows and beheld an ocean of trees in our backyard.

The last time I visited my boyhood home was in 2008 when I came back to Milwaukee to bury Mom, who died after a long illness. The owners of the home on Jonathan Lane graciously allowed me and my sister Jo to come in and wander around, but its insides had been dramatically updated. I stood in familiar rooms but had to draw on my memory to un-decorate them back to their original states. Only the outer shell remained familiar.

My memories of the original house remain in permanent but faded Kodachrome colors all those years after I last walked around inside it. The dwelling as I knew it when Mom, Dad, infant Jo, and I moved in in 1958 is gone forever, and that is as it should be. Like all things, a house changes.

I lived here and on this land for twenty-five years. The ravine surrounding the house was my playground. I never hesitated to call it my ravine. I say it in the way a boy refers to "my house" and "my yard" when they are not his property. "My" is a reference to place, to knowing that I belonged there. This was my home. The ravine was my refuge. I understand why I miss it so much today.

To a boy of eight or nine, a cul-de-sac surrounded by woods was identical to an island in the middle of an ocean: a place of adventure wrapped by the untamed wild. My cul-de-sac hovered on the precipice of such a place. When I lived there our home on the dead-end at Jonathan Lane was the private domain of only two other residences: the Rossiters and the McKnights. We, these neighbors and the Ibachs, lived on a finger of land surrounded by a lush forest.

A ravine is a unique creation in nature, and Lake Michigan was the beneficiary of many ravines on the eastern shores of Wisconsin. They are carved and sloping ecosystems home to rich collections of flora, fauna, and at their lowest point, streams. I can close my eyes and the scents of green vegetation crushed underfoot fill my nostrils. The smell is thick and fragrant, like fresh pea pods. Almost no flowering plants grow in the depths of the ravine as too little direct sunlight makes it to the ravine floor. I can also recall the soft texture of earth pressing up against the thin-soled sneakers I wore as a boy when I explored. The collection of these ravines and their flowing water purl their way to Lake Michigan. They are ancient and number about fifty, between northern Illinois and northern Wisconsin.

But I was unable to comprehend how this small forest and the streams that flowed through it framed my adoption until many years later.

To some people, children especially, a forest can be a scary place. A forest, however small, is a metaphor for a threatening environment, evil and darkness and danger, loss of control. I had no trepidations as a kid about wandering off into the woods around our house. In fact, Mom shooed me outdoors as soon as I'd had breakfast on summer mornings just to get rid of me. My siblings, too, as they grew older, although they never had the same affinity for the ravine that I did.

I remember one hot, sticky morning in July 1966. My best friend was Cliff Zieve, who lived two houses away. He and I were both nine years old, about to set off on a mission. The ravine surrounding my house was not a single ravine, but two, and by definition a ravine has a stream at its lowest point. So that meant there were two streams. Cliff and I knew about both, but we had never seen where the two streams came together. Finding that spot was our goal. What we did not know was how far we would have to travel, or what we would encounter along the way.

"Mom said we'd find it if we walked far enough," I said to Cliff the day before we set out.

"We just follow one of the streams?"

"Yup," I nodded, confident I knew what I was talking about because Mom was certain.

"How long will it take to get there?"

"Dunno," I said, honestly. "So you wanna do it?"

"Yeah."

"Be here tomorrow morning."

"You bet."

The next morning, Cliff and I stood on the threshold of my driveway. Across the street, the entrance to a theater of forest and wildlife waited patiently. We knew the way in, where the curtains of tall grasses and bramble and sprawling deciduous trees neither of us could name overlapped, like folds in a tapestry. We had studied them closely and made this trip so often, the folds seemed to part for us. The ravine was a siren out of mythology and no lashings could hold us back.

"You spray yourself?" I asked my friend. Mosquitos never bothered me much, but Mom wouldn't let me out the door without a good dousing.

"Mom sprayed me," said Cliff.

"Same here."

Cliff and I spoke little when we set off on a day of exploring and playing in the ravine. The technical term we used for our regular outings was "goofing around." Friendship at this age among boys is non-verbal, at least that's my unscientific theory. Cliff and I did not share secrets. We shared experiences. We did not talk much, but we laughed, with and at each other. Buddhists might call this "being in the moment." I called it fun. Our world was right in front of us.

The overgrown slope that led down into the ravine was steep, a severe drop from Jonathan Lane, layered in shades of green ground cover that made a foothold challenging. We slid-walked-slid, sat-on-our-behinds-then-stood-back-up, a slow-then-fast descent. Down, down, down, thirty, forty feet below street level, until at the ravine's lowest point, we regained our footing and tilted our heads up and saw the umbrella of treetops, but no hint of humanity. We were foreign creatures deep within, the only two of our kind on this day. In its lushest summer months, the ravine obscured almost entirely any hint of the homes whose yards backed up to its edges. This was a hidden world, better than a tree fort, better than a camping tent, better than a cave.

Traveling to this world below street level never made me afraid, either when I was alone or with Cliff. A place like this was dense with life, a philharmonic of animals and birds and insects that rose and fell as we moved through the ravine. I saw chipmunks and squirrels, chickadees, bluebirds, red-headed woodpeckers. I spied rabbits, the occasional deer, the rarer fox, a green snake or two, and insects that made you stop and look, and some that made you keep moving. At night raccoon eyes glimmered, fireflies danced along the edges of bushes and trees. I did not know the names of many of the creatures in the woods. What I thought were old hoot owls might have been mourning doves.

My uniform rarely changed. I plunged worry-free wearing shorts and a T-shirt, strode through knee-high undergrowth, pushed aside, bare-handed, imposing shoulder-height branches, or climbed over fallen logs. Every step we took put us amid creepy crawlies that bit, and leaves that caused rashes were everywhere, but we were junior superheroes, immune to the dangers.

Cliff and I stood less than a football field's length from my house when we reached the lowest spot below Jonathan Lane, but it felt much farther away. The difference between up there and down here was the distance between us and the moon.

I was not paying attention. Morning sun over our right shoulders angled into the depths of the ravine intermittently, blocked by tree branches. We had been in shadows, but Cliff halted us as we stepped into laser-shafts of light.

"Look," Cliff said, pointing.

A couple feet in front of us was a spider web bejeweled by dew, as broad as a Roman soldier's shield. It hovered above the ground, suspended in the air, shimmering as if to warn anyone from passing.

"Do you see the spider anywhere?" said Cliff. He was always the intrepid one and leaned in closer with the same lack of restraint as the hair his baseball cap could not contain.

"No," I said, and we studied the web's architecture. Spiders typically don't hang out in the middle of their creations, except in Saturday morning Bella Lugosi movies, but instead seek shelter on the edges of one of the supporting branches.

"It's gotta be pretty big," said Cliff, his voice filled with awe.

We did not find the designer of this artistic finery, but that was okay with me. I detested spiders, especially the large ones. We kept our distance but stood in admiration at the spider's intricate, steely matrix. We were Indiana Jones before we knew who he was.

The ravine's canopy hid an entire world beneath its latticed structure. Sunlight pinpricked its way to the ravine floor, but what it produced was precisely what made this space so inviting to us. The undergrowth smelled of green and was thick and spread out like carpeting beneath the soaring trees, but not like a jungle so that it impeded our progress. I did not know the names of most of these growing, green, brown, and pale-yellow plants, some only inches above the dark, moist earth of the ravine floor, others a foot or two in height. Cliff didn't either. But everywhere we visited within this haven, especially in the spring and early summer, lay seeds and spores and tendrils and eggs huddling in silent, confident waiting. They were the promise of the ravine's future.

Like two young versions of Lewis and Clark, with nothing but the clothes on our backs, a warm day, relaxed company, and a sense of the possible, Cliff and I were on our way to find the spot where the two streams joined up. With each step, our sneakers crunched the green things beneath them, but the sound was muffled because the amphitheater space of the ravine acted like a recording booth. We headed toward the stream a few dozen feet from the bottom of the slope we'd just descended. We heard the water before we saw it. The vegetation in early July was mature, and the moving water wended its way toward Lake Michigan. Years later, I would see on Google that it appeared snake-like, but to two boys on a day trip approaching it on foot, the stream was a playground in stereo. In some places, the waterway was two or three feet across, and the constricted flow shoved itself around smooth, fist- and softball-sized rocks, plinking like treble keys on a piano.

"Bet I can jump it without a running start," I said.

"Me, too."

CLIFF and I found the point of convergence of the two streams. When I consulted Google Maps recently, I discovered that the journey we took that hot July morning more than a half century ago covered no more than five hundred feet, but even with the twists and turns of the rill and our diversions along the way, our hiking time probably spanned two hours, there and back.

I would give anything to be my nine-year-old self again so that I could explore my ravine, splash in the cold waters of its ancient stream, and stand in my bare feet on that spot we discovered together, where two streams at the lowest points of two ravines came together, with my best friend.

Nancy Verrier spoke often about how adoptees feel like victims, that they feel powerless over their life's circumstances even as adults. I am chagrined that I ever entertained her ideas because "victim" was never a word I used to describe myself, then or now. Even the word "victimized," although it was an accurate term in a literal sense, makes me uncomfortable. I was separated from my birth mother, and I had no say in the matter. I was placed in a new home with two people I was not related to by blood. I am not superhuman, so I was not impervious to the impact of these circumstances.

All I can say is that I was never haunted by not knowing my birth mother. I never felt abandoned, I never felt rejected, I never felt that I had to prove my worthiness to be in and among the Ibach clan. These emotions never surfaced, and I am content and secure enough to say I am also convinced these emotions are not percolating beneath the surface.

It is hard to convey the utter lack of consequence and importance being an adoptee meant to me from the time I learned I was adopted until I discovered the identity of Irene, my birth mother. Some adoptees are haunted by many of the symptoms of trauma Nancy Verrier described. But my life with Mom and Dad and my siblings placed me within an unseen and powerful force field that protected me and us. We never escaped the sad and tragic events of life we saw on local television news. We had our share, like everyone else, of disappointment and heartbreak, but then we also celebrated the happy milestones of growing up. What I never suffered from was a lack of knowing where I belonged. I was never "the adopted" son. I was always and only "my number one son" to use one of Mom's favorite phrases. Even though I'm sure she meant this literally because I was in fact the first new member of the next generation of the Ibach family, I was always free to interpret it any way I chose.

The dark, scary, evil environs of a ravine were never dark or scary or evil for me. The ravine was my safe space, and today it is a soothing thought I return to often in my memories and my daily meditation. There I was in control, never afraid, never alone. The ravine was mine and I belonged to the ravine, surely the same way I belonged to the Ibach family.

I lived the life I know and was meant to know, and it was enough. I was never afraid of what I did not know. There were no shadows, no dark corners. The unlit path I would one day encounter in my search for my birth mother was a place of adventure and discovery, never a fear-filled alley, a specter to run away from.

When I die, the ravine will be my resting place, my ashes scattered there, gathered beneath the undergrowth, ready to rejoin the nurturing soil and the eternal vibrations of boyhood laughter, a final return to the one place on Earth I call home.

# 10

Dad was easy to underestimate. He called himself a plugger, which seemed an odd word coming from a man who was a straight-A student, graduated summa cum laude from the University of Wisconsin, and was invited into Phi Beta Kappa. The word *plugger* is the nominalization of the verb phrase *to plug away at*. It was in the dictionary.

When I was a child, Dad brought up the word whenever the conversation turned to school, homework, grades, chores, sports. Dad insisted that his achievements, and they were considerable, did not come naturally or effortlessly. He wanted me to know that he worked hard. He persevered. He had grit. Which, he claimed, made him a plugger. The word fit him. It fit his personality and his physique: he was short, compact, skinny when he was a teen but by middle age had filled out like a welterweight boxer or a baseball catcher. His stature was close to the ground and always gave me the sense that he was steady and steadfast. He used this word a lot around me and my siblings, and I've thought about it frequently. It was, I think, his way of downplaying his intellectual prowess while building up our own, by showing all of us that we mattered. In other words, what a good father does.

Dad was unpretentious. He was also a little nerdy. For years he wore horn-rimmed glasses, thin bow ties, and a Johnny Unitas flattop haircut. His tight-lipped smile, a product of his self-consciousness about crooked teeth, seemed to diminish his natural warmth by a degree or two until you got to know him. It contributed to his taciturn nature. But it gave him the appearance of an academic.

As a physician, he'd tell you that writing was not his forte. I have saved all his letters, and I can testify that my dad was telling the truth. He was not a writer, not in the way most people think about what it means to be a writer. His sentences were declarative, formal, matter of fact. He wrote the way Star Trek's Mr. Spock spoke: no contractions. The results were functional, without a hint of irony or humor or nuance. It was not bad writing. It was simply not memorable.

But he taught me the mechanics of writing, and I have always been embarrassed by the way it happened. Today I understand his method, even if he wasn't aware of it. Perhaps he was. He reminds me now of Mr. Miyagi from *The Karate Kid*, who showed Daniel how to "sand the floor" as he taught his charge the basics of karate. Dad taught by demonstrating, not by lecturing. It was serious old school.

What did he do that caused me such angst? Dad wrote my papers for me, for a short span of my elementary school life at any rate. Then he instructed me to copy, word for word in my own hand, exactly what he had written. He never explained why he wanted me to do this. He simply wrote my essay assignments, some short, some long, in his own neat handwriting, handed over the yellow legal pad to me, and said, "Now go to your room and write it out just as I've written it."

I shared this story with a writing mentor, the late novelist and playwright Richard Setlowe, assuming he would be sympathetic and make a joke about it. Instead, he matter-of-factly convinced me that my dad had been a teacher, a competent one at that. My embarrassment, my shame, had been misplaced.

Then I realized there was never an ounce of judgment or

ridicule or shaming from him when he did this. His tone was always even-keeled and encouraging. My embarrassment came later when I awoke to the implications of what he had done. The conclusion I drew was that he did this for me because I was incapable of doing it for myself.

Perhaps my reluctance to admit that he did my homework lies in a deep-seated fear that its revelation would be like a scarlet letter and hasten my ridicule. Or maybe it would diminish in the minds of others whatever reputation I had for academic success.

Sometimes when he did my homework, I made boyish decisions I came to regret. My sixth-grade teacher gave us a challenging, and what turned out to be a long, assignment, at least by my youthful standards. We were to write a five- or six-page paper on any explorer we chose, and I picked Vasco da Gama. It was a doorstopper of a tome from my perspective.

The mistake I made was costly because I copied only as many of Dad's paragraphs as I was in the mood to transcribe, either because I was tired, or because I resented what he'd done. My unfaithfulness produced a lower grade. It turned out that every paragraph had its purpose. What I chose to leave out broke the natural flow of the narrative. My eleven-year-old self could not grasp this abstraction, and the result was the equivalent of sinking one of da Gama's ships.

It was an early form of rebellion. Some kids dropped acid. I dropped paragraphs.

But I learned how to write. In the same way student painters learn brush strokes, or how to achieve chiaroscuro, or create depth, and manipulate color by copying the works of the masters of painting, I learned the basics of writing by copying my dad's.

A few years before he died, I reminded him of this episode of my education, and he laughed.

"I wrote a lot of papers for you kids," he said, without taking any credit for his influence.

He was no master, but he was more teacher than he ever

admitted. I lived a lot of years before it dawned on me that, like Dad, I too was a plugger. He planted the seed.

I recall this singular episode in my life without feeling a hint of trauma because Dad was not my biological father. Teaching me the subtle art of writing papers was a gift, one that my writing mentor pointed out to me decades after the fact, given to me by the man who was my dad.

## 11

My memories of Mom are not chronological. Little snippets, like short film clips that play in my head, return to me unbidden. Mom's foibles and peccadilloes and most charming idiosyncrasies come to mind—especially, but not always, the ones that make me smile.

Martha Joyce Mendenhall Ibach was a garden of contradictions. In other words, she was normal. She died in 2008 after nine years of cancer and Alzheimer's, so my family and I were robbed of a moment to say goodbye. A body remained long after Mom departed.

She was a Goldwater Republican who purchased phosphate-free laundry detergent because she cared about the environment, years, decades, before it was popular. On at least two separate occasions, both before I reached twelve, she invited a homeless pregnant teen to live with us until the young girls gave birth and offered their infants for adoption. She was a scientist with a degree in bacteriology as well as a woman of faith, although she kept quiet about it except to attend church every Sunday. She never talked politics that I recall, yet she ran for president of the school board where I and my siblings attended. And won. Twice.

Mom did what all the mothers of my friends did: she was

there for me when I needed her, and she made me cringe, sometimes at the same moment.

One of my earliest recollections of a cringe moment is when Mom turned down a chance to own a Mercedes. What a thing to do to a teenage boy. When I was fourteen, Dad drove Mom and me to a Mercedes-Benz dealership where Mom test-drove a two-door Mercedes coupe, an expensive model. But that's not saying much. All Mercedes Benzes were expensive, then and today. She'd dreamed of owning this vehicle and to the extent that I paid attention to the wants and desires of my parents, I was vaguely aware of this aspiration. I tagged along because I loved looking at and sitting in new cars. And, well, there was also the possibility of seeing the little rocket in front of our house.

While Mom was out driving the coupe, Dad and I remained at the dealership. The car was a two-seater, and this was Mom's party. The test-drive didn't last long. When Mom stepped out of her dream Mercedes, she was frowning.

"The sound of the motor hurts my ears," she said.

Driving age was within my grasp and I was crushed. Dad was undoubtedly relieved. There would be no Benz in our driveway.

Mom and Dad wore their growing prosperity gingerly, as if it were a size too large, but with pride at the hard work it required and humility it took. They were humble people. I started to realize, years later, that Mom may have felt she would be uncomfortable in such a showy symbol of status. I suspect that she found a physical ailment to cover her mixed feelings.

"Oh, I love this car," I imagined her saying, "but it's just not who I am."

As an adolescent at the time, I fantasized about one day showing off this hot machine to all my friends. Now, decades later, I can hear Mom saying *"but it's not who I am"* even though she never actually said it, not to me, not out loud. Mom's experience with the Mercedes was the first time I saw a tangible example of the difference between wanting and having.

If she could not bring herself to say some things, other things

I wished, as a youth, she had not said at all. The way she answered the telephone, for example.

"This is Martha."

"Hi, Mom."

"Well, if it isn't my number one son ..."

Mom never said "Hello" the way Dad did. The way every other human being on the planet did, or so I thought.

For such a simple phrase, Mom made it unforgettable. She said "This" on a down-note, then "is" on an up-note, and ended on "Mar-tha" as a double-note between the two. The result was a four-syllable melody that never changed. It was her trademark.

In high school, when my buddies called me at home, often to reach Mom and her cheery solo, they found endless ways to ridicule me about her telephone greeting.

Some of my buddies mimicked her in return to identify themselves. Mom always played along. One or two told me they were charmed by the encounter. Others mocked her. I heard many variations when they finally got me on the phone. It entertained them immensely and only mildly irritated me.

I never pleaded with Mom to be like other mothers and just say "Hello" when she picked up the phone. I could have, but I didn't.

More than two decades have passed since I have heard "This is Martha," except in my head. I can hear her voice as if she had just answered the phone, a four-note ditty I dream about.

WHEN MOM DIED, I was not with her the way I would be with Dad many years later.

At her memorial service, I told stories that I remembered from growing up.

One story became family legend. When my siblings and I were in elementary school, we practically lived in front of our console television in the downstairs family room of our home in Bayside. As soon as we returned from school, the sofa in front of the TV was our singular destination. We parked there and wouldn't move until dinner some two hours later. Mom used to say that I watched enough TV by the time I started high school to fill three lifetimes.

When the four of us were old enough to know which shows we liked and which we didn't, battles ensued over the remote control and the channel. As the oldest, I usually won these battles, and *Star Trek*, *Dragnet*, and *Wagon Train* topped the list. Whether my siblings liked these choices is debatable, but the one advantage I discovered about being the oldest: I didn't care.

Nor did I care much when Mom called us upstairs for dinner. We routinely ignored her repeated calls. I don't know if my siblings truly enjoyed what we were watching, if they chose to follow my lead and ignore her, if they weren't hungry, or a little of all three. The reality was none of us budged.

This act of defiance was a nightly routine, a kind of bad re-run my mother endured. I have no recollection of how long this went on. But I know the length of Mom's fuse.

What I never forgot was the turning point. Call it a slow lava-flow eruption.

One afternoon, in the middle of *Star Trek*, the four of us — some sitting on the sofa, others on the floor in front of it — had a group experience that was as if Wisconsin had been pummeled by an earthquake, an event I am certain has never occurred in post-ice-age history.

The ground wasn't moving. Mom was. We could hear her footsteps from above. They made their way across the ceiling, then to the stairwell behind us, then pounded down each step like an approaching avalanche. At the bottom of the stairs, she turned toward the television and did not stop. Only in passing did I notice a shiny object in her left hand. When she reached the TV, I thought she'd simply slap the switch to turn it off and then address us in a hellion tirade.

That would have been expected and preferred. That's not what happened. Instead, she committed an act that went down in

Ibach family infamy. She reached behind the television and yanked out the electric cord connecting the television to the wall socket with such a controlled, swift elegance, we barely had time to react. Electric cord in hand, the shiny object she held, which turned out to be a pair of scissors, descended on the dangling prong end of the cord and she cut off the plug. One easy motion, like a sharp voice through the din. The television was not just turned off. It was terminated.

We didn't move. We were too stunned to move. What we'd just witnessed was far more dramatic than anything we'd been watching. You could almost hear Mr. Spock say, "Fascinating ..." My sister, Linda, summed up the scene with a foreboding beyond her years.

"Wow," she said. "Wait till Daddy finds out."

M OM  WITNESSED the drowning death of her first-born son, my younger brother, Mike, in April 1980.

Though I was not there when my brother died, I can see it in my imagination. I can see Mom on the sandy beach of Oconomowoc Lake, where she and Dad had purchased a home only months earlier, about thirty minutes west of where we grew up in Bayside. She would have been bundled in winter boots and clothing as Mike sat in the beached canoe and pleaded with her to let him take it out on the lake.

"You have no paddle," she said, impatiently.

"Moooom," he insisted in a monotone whine. "I want to take the canoe out."

"Okay, okay," she lamented. "Just wait. I'll get the paddle."

What did Mike look like on this, his last day? When I flipped through an old family photo album, I came across a snapshot of Mike standing on the rippled blue-white ice of Oconomowoc Lake, perhaps two hundred feet offshore. Dad likely took the photo. I saw no hand-written caption on the back, but there was a computer-generated time stamp that read February 1980. He was facing west because the sun made him squint. The light was fading, so it must have been late afternoon. He wore a knit cap, a hooded winter parka, gloves, his aviator glasses, and the familiar crooked smile.

In my imagining, Mom walked-ran the half-football-field-length lawn up to the house to retrieve the paddle, but by the time she returned, a bone-chilling late winter gust had un-beached the canoe and sent it across the gray, white-capped water, away from the house. I try to imagine the sight of her, on the edge of the pier that poked into Oconomowoc Lake's waters about fifty feet, paddle in hand. The canoe had blown at least a thousand feet offshore, moving away from her.

Mom yelled and I can almost see her face, an image that presaged the inevitable tragedy. She could not have known what was to come.

"Stay in the canoe, Mike!" she screamed. "Stay in the canoe! Until it reaches the other side of the lake!"

Mike was eighteen and would be nineteen in two days. He was developmentally disabled, a deficiency that left him vulnerable. It is unlikely that he heard the screams of his mother. Or if he had, he was unable to make sense of the words.

He panicked. He jumped out of the canoe and tried to swim back to shore. But April in Wisconsin meant the lake had only recently thawed. The water temperature was in the forties. Michael John was fully dressed including a heavy winter coat, knit cap and gloves. And boots.

My mother stood on land. No probably knee-deep, waist-deep, in the frigid lake. Held back by the police officer she had called by then, screaming at the top of her lungs. Clawing to escape the officer's grip in her attempt to swim out to him. Begging the officer to let her go. Begging Mike to stay in the canoe until it drifted all the way across the lake.

My almost, but not quite, never-to-be nineteen-year-old brother drowned. In the presence of his mother. Who carried the burden of that guilt and responsibility to her death.

A tragedy like this one tears apart some marriages. Mom and Dad carried on. Mom never stopped referring to me as her "number one son" even though Mike was, in fact, her first naturally born child. I never had to think, much less worry, about this truth. That day in April 1980, the Ibach family—my family—lost one of its members. We all lost a piece of ourselves that day. We all carried on, together, just as Mom and Dad did.

At Mike's funeral services, I sat behind Mom and Dad in the church. When I stood to deliver Mike's eulogy, I noticed that Dad had his portable cassette player/recorder on the pew next to him. He was recording everything. I am certain it was not his idea. I am certain Mom asked him to make the recording. I asked him once, a year later, if she ever listened to it.

"No," he said, looking up from his newspaper.

"Why did she want it?"

He looked down at his newspaper. "Just to have it."

We never talked about it again.

## 12

Until the COVID-19 pandemic shut down daily life in Los Angeles in 2020, I used to take a Sunday morning yoga class at Studio A Dance on Hyperion Avenue. This place was an institution in my neighborhood of Silver Lake, my home since 2016, when I moved out of the apartment I'd shared with Zoe. The class occupied a spacious, light-filled room with a high ceiling and an opaque skylight shrouded partially by a ripped piece of canvas and mirrors covering the longest wall.

Despite the instructor's diligent sweeping before class, however, the floor was covered with bits of sequins, sparkle and glitter that fell from attire worn by young ballet dancers, who took classes here during the week. The debris was everywhere, mostly unseen by the naked eye. When I placed my midnight blue yoga mat on the dance floor, called a Marley surface because it is thick and absorbs a dancer's pounding, specks of this detritus found their way to my mat, creating on the rectangular shape an amphitheater of the night sky with tiny stars twinkling back at me as I moved from child's pose to tabletop to down dog to a lunge. At the end of class, I rolled up the mat and stowed it in its carrier. When I unrolled it again and I began the routines of my practice in a different class a couple days later, I found the Carl Sagan-like cosmos in miniature had remained largely intact on my yoga mat, lying flat against the studio floor. Stars made up no constellations I recognized, yet they winked at me. They were my own private galaxy.

No matter how hard I tried, I could not remove the sparkle and glitter that adhered to my yoga mat. After many unsuccessful cleanings, I gave up. I decided that I liked the effect. I liked to take in this dark surface now dotted with reflective material that produced no harmful effects to my body.

My glimmering yoga mat reminded me, every time I unrolled it, of how much mental junk I carried around each day that did not belong to me. Like pilot fish that nestle up to a shark, feeding off the remains of its kills, my yoga mat clued me in to how much psychic baggage I'd collected often without being aware of it— some of it my own worries and fears, much of it acquired from family, friends, the nightly news. Someone I'd met a few years earlier brought me out of this fog and taught me how to be more mindful.

Los Angeles was my home on two separate occasions. The first time from 1993 to 2003, and then a job took me to Minneapolis. Then another job took me to Jersey City, NJ in 2010. Over a twenty-six-year career in advertising I lived in five different cities. In the late spring of 2012, I came back to Los Angeles, but now I was an educator, not an advertising creative. I taught English and literature at three LA community colleges.

A month after my return to Los Angeles, I re-joined my old gym in Hollywood and started a ninety-minute workout each day, six days a week. One morning I heard words that still echo in my head.

"Good morning, young man."

This greeting was spoken by a man I knew then only as Michael. He said it to almost everyone he encountered. We saw each other at the gym, where we both were members. He was just another gym rat, like so many of the regulars I saw every day.

The gym was filled with some of the hulkiest, be-muscled

human beings I have ever seen, but Michael was different. Even in his knit skull cap, long-sleeved shirt worn under a short-sleeved shirt, dark sweatpants, and black weight-lifting gloves, Michael's diminutive stature seemed only to enhance his magnetic presence. Grunting through a set, he couldn't hide his photogenic smile. Members and trainers often came up to say something or gave a friendly wave as they walked by. This gym was known for a handful of celebrity members. I said hello to Wilson Cruz, whom I'd met years earlier, and Ron Perlman, best known for his roles in the television series *Beauty and the Beast* and *Sons of Anarchy*. To be honest, Ron scared me a little. He wasn't imposing, but that scowl. Someone should have turned it into a Halloween mask. And I never called him Ron to his face, always Mr. Perlman.

I also knew that some members had been around for decades. Many friendships started here. Michael seemed like a popular fellow and in those early days of what I called LA 2.0, I did not know who and what he was. But there was something oddly familiar about him, as if I knew him—but of course I did not know him.

He stood five-seven with a beaming oval face, ears hidden by the mid-back-length dreadlocks, which gave him the ethereal aura of a poet. One morning, Michael and I bumped into each other as we were leaving. We walked together on the sidewalk on Cole Avenue toward the parking lot.

"You know, Michael," I said, "I don't know anything about you. What do you do?"

It was an all-too-typical question, but I had to start somewhere.

"I'm the founder and spiritual director of Agape International Spiritual Center," he said matter-of-factly.

My forehead deserved a good smacking. He was Reverend Dr. Michael Bernard Beckwith. I'd never seen a photo of him before, but I'd certainly heard about him and Agape. Some friends had brought up both names when I lived in LA in the late 90s. I had thought about going to a service but never managed to get there.

Michael never bugged me about attending Agape. Not once. But one thing changed: I stopped calling him Michael. He became Reverend Michael, or more often simply Rev.

For a year after meeting Rev at the gym, I grew accustomed to hearing "Good morning, young man" when I saw him. But I still had not found my way to Agape for Sunday services.

And then Zoe came into my life in 2014. She was a practicing Buddhist, who meditated and chanted daily. I told her about seeing and chatting with Reverend Michael every time she and I were together.

"Do you want to go?" she asked me one Saturday afternoon when I was hanging out at her apartment.

"What, you mean Agape?"

"Yeah, you talk about Reverend Michael all the time."

"Okay, sure. When?"

"Let's go tomorrow."

Zoe had been to Agape. I told her that I'd had opportunities to attend years earlier but didn't.

"A friend urged me to go," I said to her. "She said Agape was known as a target-rich environment for single women."

"And now you're bringing sand to the beach," she said, laughing. I think she was laughing at me, but I didn't mind.

Zoe's apartment was only a few minutes from Agape's Culver City location in those days. We arrived for the 11:30 a.m. services. As we waited outside for the 9 a.m. service to end, the exterior of the building, which was a nondescript two-story warehouse with picture windows around its lobby entry, gave me no hint of what I would find inside. Zoe had been here before, so she knew what to expect.

The line we joined snaked around the parking lot, doubling back on itself. Agape staff had anticipated this and had set up ropes as guides. I hadn't noticed right away, but three separate doorways led into the sanctuary. When the doors opened, one was for those inside to exit. After a few minutes, the other two were opened for those of us waiting to enter.

Agape is not a "megachurch," even though it's huge and has showed up on online lists of megachurches. That word is typically associated with a Christian church and Agape was neither Christian nor a church. But I soon discovered that Agape regulars do in fact call Agape a church even though it's a "spiritual center." It was easier and less complicated when we talked among ourselves.

But I did not have to attend many times before I began to understand the difference between a traditional church and Agape. I've attended churches that described themselves as non-denominational. Agape went further and called itself omni-denominational. Agape covered everything and everyone from A to Z: from atheism to Zoroastrianism. A few atheists declared themselves, but I can't say if any Zoroastrians attended. Yet.

The Agape sanctuary was bigger than any two high school gymnasiums and seated about a thousand people. At the far end of the space, opposite from where we entered, a stage emerged from the floor, about three steps up, lit with professionally hung kliegs and spots. The stage was carpeted and trunk-sized amplification speakers, facing away from the audience, lined the front edge. On the far-left side, cordoned off in a space of its own, was the area reserved for what I learned was called the Agape House Band. The size and number of speakers told me this was no church combo.

I'd attended more than a few Black worship services and at first, I thought Agape would be like the others. But no, Agape was different. As I scanned the space, I saw a sea of color, from clothing to hats to hair to skin tones. Rev called Agape the United Nations. There were American Indians in full headgear, with beads and feathers down to the floor. Men and women in a candy-store variety of head wraps. Brightly colored silk and wool and other fabric around shoulders and waists, sewn as skirts and floor-length dresses and slacks. African tribal patterns. Indian and Middle Eastern and Asian. Later I met and befriended a few gay men and although I didn't say anything, I marveled that the more fashion-forward had their work cut out for them on a Sunday morning at Agape. And if you cared at all about footwear, Agape was a haven for Nordstrom shoe-sale addicts.

This was all surface stuff. Yet it made a deeply moving and positive first impression.

Like other Black church experiences in my life, Agape's shared a couple features in common. First and foremost, music. Lots of it. And since we were in Los Angeles, it was of the highest caliber. The Agape International Spiritual Choir was an audition-only volunteer organization. It recorded and it traveled. Even the most nervous-looking soloist who'd step forward from the wall of singers lined up at the back of the stage belted out a song like her name was Aretha.

Second, Agape was about hugs and getting physical. If you were not comfortable hugging and high-fiving you stayed home and watched the services online, what we in the Agape Nation called Love Streaming. "Agape Nation" and "Love Streaming" were just a few of the new vocabulary words I learned. There were many more.

After that first service, Zoe and I walked out through the lobby and to the curb where we found Reverend Michael greeting worshippers.

"Rev," I said, shaking his hand and chuckling a bit. I was not accustomed to seeing him in his Sunday-go-to-meeting finest. "I'd like you to meet Zoe."

He took her hand and said hello.

"Did you bring him?" he asked.

"Yes," she said, her face glowing. I don't know why I was surprised Rev would ask her that.

The date was October 12, 2014, about eighteen months after I met Reverend Michael at the gym.

I LEARNED a lot about Rev in the years I've known him, but one quality stands out: he is a patient man.

"I plant seeds," he liked to say.

He was never pushy, never a proselytizer, far more an educator than a preacher, even though preaching was what he did. I'd call him a treacher, which I think he might like. He was always making up words, although he was more adept at it than I was. Bliscipline was one of his favorites—the discipline of your spiritual practices leads to bliss. He served up a gourmet buffet every week. Gorge yourself, pick at it, fast, or ignore it altogether. That was our choice and our business. Agape was not about dogma. Agape was about consciousness, realization, service, first to your highest self because you couldn't serve others if you didn't know why you were on the planet. Only then could you help someone else.

But I'm not selling here. I found a home and a family and a set of spiritual practices that became part of my life. Long before I met Reverend Michael or attended Agape, I already believed in a divine presence. My faith was strong, although I knew that the "roots" of my beliefs were planted in soft ground. Agape firmed me up.

Rev also helped prepare me for the journey that led me to Irene, my birth mother. He didn't point in any direction or advise me on how to take the journey itself. That was my work. Rev did what he does best and planted seeds. I nurtured them with my spiritual practices.

I came to Agape out of curiosity. I was not interested in scripture or finding a savior or seeking after an anthropomorphic figure in the sky or a heaven that was out there, somewhere in a distant future. When Rev said, "What God does is reveal Itself as each of us," I knew I had found my spiritual home, with like-minded brothers and sisters.

I saw and talked to Reverend Michael many days during the week when we worked out together at the gym, a privilege I have always treasured and never took for granted. Even if I could say only, "Morning Rev," and he'd reply, "Brother Howard!" it felt like an extra blessing.

I dove in, too. I attended Agape-sponsored classes—one on meditation was taught by Reverend Michael. The word around Agape, from other ministers as well as regulars, was that Rev was an in-demand "master" meditation teacher, who traveled all over the world leading seminars and workshops on meditation skills. Zoe was a daily meditator, so I sat most mornings in my own awkward fashion after I started attending Agape. That led me to Rev's class.

In time, I took advantage of the new ways to serve in my community. One easy way to dip my toe in was through Agape's annual Sacred Service Saturday, but I was already committed to serving others before I found Agape. For many years, I was a volunteer writing teacher for InsideOUT Writers and taught Saturday morning classes in LA Juvenile Hall. And I was a regular English tutor at the community colleges where I taught.

I went on my first weekend-long silent meditation retreat, a celebration to bring in the New Year, which Agape holds in late December in the desert in Joshua Tree near Palm Springs. I signed up for another meditation retreat the following spring in the high desert north of Los Angeles.

"Don't believe everything you think!" Rev said often on Sunday mornings. It was one of his favorite phrases, and mine.

I heard it as a call to examine my thinking, a kind of meta-thinking exercise. Be aware of what rattles around inside my head to make sure the things I believe are what I truly believe. Are they *my* thoughts? Or did I appropriate them? They could come from family, friends, television, newspapers, Hollywood, graffiti on a wall, social media. It was okay if my thinking was influenced by someone or something else, so long as I questioned my beliefs and claimed ownership of them. If they didn't pass muster, I'd toss 'em out.

Like the glitter on my yoga mat, I had to be vigilant and decipher which of my thoughts were truly my own and which were not. Rev was an insightful teacher.

For example, because my birth mother surrendered me for adoption, the idea I could easily and understandably have carried in my head was that I had been *rejected* at birth. In a literal sense, this could be called a fact. She did not want me or could not keep me for reasons I did not know. These were early days in my emerging awareness of the research around adoption. And it was long before I ever set eyes on my adoption report, which would offer some oblique but intriguing explanations.

Another false belief: because I remained incurious about my adoption from childhood well into adulthood, it could be interpreted that I hid from the idea that "I was rejected." This could be part of the "primal wound," and like a knife plunged deeply into my psyche, it was inflicted on me before I was verbal or conscious, long before I was equipped to question it or push back. But to accept that "I was rejected," and to believe it as truth, I would be denying that I possessed the tools to overcome the wound, tools I knew I had within my power. What Irene chose in 1956 had nothing to do with who I am today.

I wish I could say that I arrived at these thoughts right away and never considered the notion that I had been rejected. I can't. What I can say is that Rev's teaching was a powerful weapon in my first line of defense and armed me with enough clear thinking to reinforce what I already possessed. The fiction of *rejection* lacked penetrating power. My adoptive family, I reminded myself, had coated me with what I called Love Teflon: no thought of "I was rejected" would ever stick.

False beliefs, Rev said, became personal narratives *by choice.* They either dictated me or I dictated them. The choice to accept or reject the ideas and opinions I have accumulated about myself rested solely with me. I must be discriminating.

His words, whether on a Sunday morning or in private, brief chats at the gym during the week, often felt like a homework assignment. I responded eagerly. The path I followed brought me to the truth about my origins, derived from within. Rev had planted the seeds about a purposeful review of my thinking. Those seeds grew and blossomed.

Very early on, Nancy Verrier's Primal Wound Theory was a powerful counterview from a so-called expert who challenged my lived experience. I had reason to be skeptical, not of the trauma itself but of its consequences and my responses to it. Now, with Rev's guidance, I was waking up to who I was all along.

## 13

"Just wanted you to know Wisconsin has passed open records for adopted [sic]. My [adopted] friend met her sister yesterday. If you would like I can send the link. MJ"

MJ was my sister Mary Jo, whom I called Jo. Her text arrived on March 26, 2017. And the timing was spooky. A week before Jo sent it, I had finally completed reading the second of two seminal textbooks on adoption by Nancy Verrier. I'd needed eighteen months to slog my way through them. But by March 19, I closed the second book at last, proud of myself for having the resilience and the tenacity to finish it.

Jo texted me seven days later with her news.

I believe in signs. *That* was a sign. The universe was speaking to me.

All Wisconsin adoptions were "closed" until 2016, when legislation was passed allowing adoptees to learn the identity of deceased birth parents. Finding your birth mother prior to that time required either a court order or that you hire a modern-day Sherlock Holmes. Both avenues likely required no small amount of money.

With Jo's text, I stood in front of a new door, a door I never expected to pass through. It was not open, yet. But the key was available to me for a mere $40 made out to the State of Wisconsin and one completed form. Three days later, on March 29, my sister sent me the link.

"I sent off my adoption search application today," I texted Jo on May 3. "We'll share notes in a few weeks."

Jo and I were my adoptive parents' first two children. She was adopted in 1958 from a different birth mother than mine, two years after I arrived. Jo had talked about finding her birth mother for as long as I can remember. I don't recall her explaining to me why she had this burning desire, only that the desire was there.

Her plan always left me feeling lukewarm: I was interested, but not motivated. When she talked about searching, I listened to her in case she made some salient point that I had not considered. She never did, but I still paid attention when she brought up the subject.

IT TOOK me twenty-nine days from the time I had access to the online application Jo had texted me to post the completed form and a check. In some things, I move slowly. My state of mind during March and April 2017 was a combination of curiosity about my past tinged with hesitation. This new-found inquisitiveness felt odd, like finding nooks in a table I had never explored, or a drawer I had not pulled open. What would I find?

If the Wisconsin Department of Children and Families could track down my adoption records, I would have answers to questions I had never even thought to ask. I should have composed a page filled with questions I wanted answered, but I did not. I was just beginning to think about what I might learn. My long-dormant adoption bug was not yet fully awake.

So, I let the post office do its work with my application and personal check and sat back to wait for the State of Wisconsin to reply. Would I be prepared for what they sent me? There was hardly reason to be anxious, none to panic. Wisconsin, after all, would not post my birth mother in the mail.

Instead, I thought, I would receive some bureaucrat's formulaic, stiff, uninspired prose.

What arrived on May 23 took my breath away.

## 14

"I am very sorry to inform you, but your birth mother passed away in August of 1976."

I stared at these words. They arrived in an email from Kerry Lenzendorf, Adoption Search Specialist, Department of Children and Families. She was writing from Madison, Wisconsin.

So: I had a birth mother, which I knew before I sent my application and check to Madison. But now I knew her name—Irene McCrackin. And she had been dead for forty-one years.

I remember feeling like someone with a split personality. My initial reaction was visceral: Wait! No! She's dead? Oh, no, she's *dead*.

But then reality kicked in. I remembered what the application form said in plain English: the State of Wisconsin would not send me anything related to my adoption records if one or both of my birth parents were alive. The adoption report-request form asked me to write an "Outreach Statement to Birth Parents" explaining my reason for seeing the report, which Wisconsin would forward to one or both birth parents in the event they were still living.

Kerry had responded to my written application only a few

weeks after I submitted it because neither of my birth parents was alive.

Irene was dead and had been for a long time. I was nineteen when she died.

There was more:

"Her obituary doesn't note how or why [she died]," Kerry continued in her May 23 email. "Also, I included the obituary for your birth mother's first husband. You will see that you have 2 half siblings too."

Siblings?

Whoa. Why hadn't I considered that possibility? I didn't know, but I felt something—delight, joy—for the first time since I opened Kerry's email.

A smile emerged on my face. No that isn't quite right. I wore a full-on shit-ass grin. I had something entirely new: older sisters. Half-sisters, yes, but sisters. This from a guy who was used to being the oldest.

Kerry's email contained two obituaries, one for Irene, my birth mother, published in 1976 and the other obituary was for her late first husband, who died in 1955. Irene's obituary said she left behind a husband, Berlon McCrackin, so she had been married at least twice. And Kerry mentioned that I had two half-siblings, Susan, and Jayne. Their names were listed as survivors in Eulo Small, Jr.'s obituary, Irene's first husband.

I breathed and took stock: my birth mother was dead. Was her widower, Berlon McCrackin, still alive? If he was alive, he'd be in his early nineties. Nothing in the email answered that question. Irene's first husband, Eulo, was dead, too. First husband. Second husband. Siblings.

And what about those odd names...Eulo? Berlon? When I was a kid, I disliked the name Howard for a minute and wondered why Mom and Dad had picked it. If I'd known about "Eulo" and "Berlon" back then, I might have thought differently.

Not the same as the arduous task of acquainting myself with the characters in *War and Peace*, but when all I had expected to read about was a birth mother, possibly a birth father, suddenly the cast was much larger than I imagined.

Irene's first husband Eulo: was he my birth father? No, he couldn't be. He died more than a year before I was born, according to his obituary. I may have been an English major, but I knew how human biology works.

What about Berlon McCrackin? He was Irene's second husband, according to her obituary, but there was no additional information about him anywhere, not in the email, not in the PDF. I knew nothing about him. He was a blank slate.

Could he be my birth father? There was no clear evidence in the few materials Kerry had sent me, and the chances that he was still living seemed slim.

My sister Jo gave me a clue. In her adoption report from Wisconsin, she found exactly what I had found: her birth father was not named either. He was as much a mystery to her as mine was to me.

"She was a teenager when she got pregnant," Jo said about her birth mother. "Her family sent her to live with relatives in Minnesota until she gave birth to me. My birth father was just a one-night thing."

Jo's story was unusual for the young women in the 1950s who became pregnant before they were married. I read Ann Fessler's *The Girls Who Went Away: The Hidden History of Women Who Surrendered Children for Adoption in the Decades before Roe v. Wade*, published in 2006. Mothers of that era who chose adoption for their newborns, according to Fessler, were often in their midtwenties, already had children and were married or widows.

That picture matched the little I knew about Irene from what Kerry had sent me: Irene was twenty-six when she had me and was the mother of two young girls, Susan and Jayne. But I did not have any information about when she had married Berlon, only that she died while married to him.

The PDF attached to the email included an old photograph of

the woman who gave birth to me sixty years earlier. She was forty-six years old when she died.

The copy of the newspaper obit's photo was a reproduction of a copy of an original, so the image blurred to a fuzzy, soft focus: Her round face, the Mona Lisa smile, eyes that hinted of a happiness that might come, or already had, but not on the day this photo was taken. Her hair was in a 1940s bob, her skin unwrinkled, the dark dress, the pearls around her neck.

Where was the likeness? The image was taken in 1947 when she was eighteen. She was so young. I have lived longer than the woman who was my birth mother, but who gave me up when I was an infant. And I was looking at a photograph of her now for the first time.

What I wanted was for her to come alive and explain why she gave me up. But she was mute, just like me, as I stared at her staring back at me. We were intimately connected, yet complete strangers. She had known me. I never knew her.

My feelings were a mash-up of emotions. I felt relief that I finally had an image of this woman. Excitement raced through me because the mystery was revealed, even though at that moment I could not know how much more was to come. The buzzing feeling was accompanied by confusion because a revelation I expected did not arrive—I did not see an obvious, unmistakable likeness in the old photograph, and this brought confusion. This is my mother? Is this my mother? Was I supposed to see myself in 1940s drag? Certainly, I thought, I was being too literal, too concrete in my expectations. But my confusion was laced with a sprig of joy because I had new siblings. The mystery was no longer a mystery and the short wait had ended, but what, exactly, did it all add up to?

I gave myself a moment to take it all in.

Something happened between the time I received the email and the time I opened it and sped-read the email's message and the attached PDF. In that short span of seconds, the questions about Irene, about her past, her thinking, her decision, came flooding into my brain. Questions I never contemplated. Questions that never needed asking. Questions that now prodded me for answers.

I started asking, as I stared at the old photograph, who are you? What were you thinking when you found out you were pregnant with me? What were you thinking when you decided to put me up for adoption? Did you make the decision quickly or did you struggle with it? What did you feel on the day I was taken from your arms? *How did you get through it?*

These questions had never entered my brain once, not once, until this day. Something else jolted me: I wasn't asking anything about me, about how she might have felt about me as I grew inside her. Instead, I was wildly curious about *her*, about her state of mind, about her emotions, about her frailties.

I jetted back in my mind to Verrier's books, and I wondered how she'd react to my thinking. I'm certain I did not fit her profile of the traumatized adoptee. What's that stale old joke about the self-absorbed guy on a date who says, "I've talked enough about myself, what do you think about me?" I was not thinking about me. I was more interested in Irene.

I did not know if I'd ever uncover the answers about my birth mother, but I was stunned, rocked back in my chair, by the hold these questions had on me. It was as if a dusty old switch had been flipped on.

I marveled at my abrupt change of heart about these details. My about-face was not instant, but once Jo had sent me her text two months earlier alerting me to the possibility that there were questions waiting to be asked and possible answers to these questions, I was on an unstoppable glide path. I don't think I could have halted my journey if I had wanted to. But then I didn't want to. As George Watson had done more than sixty years before, I set the next phase of my adoption in motion. The difference was, I was an active player in these events. I had a choice this time.

And even though at this early stage I was more focused on and fascinated by the woman who was my birth mother, in time I would start to ask new questions and those questions addressed what Irene felt about me throughout her long wait to give birth and then let me go. These questions I knew I would never find answers to, but they would bubble up. Verrier said that adoptees feel anger toward their birth mothers for abandoning them. For decades, I had never felt that anger, but I wondered, even worried, whether anger or resentment would emerge.

Kerry was right. The obituary was sparse, a classic "who, what, where, when, but not why" piece of journalism. Exactly four paragraphs. Eighty-seven words. And a too-small-to-read image of Irene's grave marker. She was born. She died.

Was there more?

Kerry promised to send my complete adoption report by email later in the week, followed by a hard copy of everything by snail mail.

## 15

If Kerry Lenzendorf's first email was a desert of information, her second email was a hurricane. It arrived on May 25, two days after she informed me that my birth mother Irene died in 1976. This new email contained my complete adoption report.

When I opened the attachment—a PDF labeled simply "Howard Ibach"—I thought it might be a few pages at most, some official forms, and maybe a few paragraphs with biographical information about my birth mother. Mostly dry facts. The fragments big and small of one's life.

What I found overwhelmed me. The document was not a couple pages, but more than thirty-three pages. I began to read, and the words seemed like they would not end. Line after line, paragraph after paragraph, page after page. On it went. Many of them single-spaced typewritten.

At first, I scrolled slowly but then faster. The more I scrolled, the more I *could* scroll, like those websites with no bottom. I scrolled through single-spaced documents, some upside down. I saw doctor's notes, the kind they scribbled in a sloppy hand after a baby was delivered. The notes were about me. Followed by more single-spaced pages, this time reporting on the first months of my life with my adoptive parents. Then courtroom transcripts where a judge asked a woman, my birth mother, if she understood that by putting me up for adoption, she would become a "legal stranger."

A *legal stranger*. It's an inelegant phrase that means she signed away her rights as a mother.

I closed the PDF. This was too much. I shut my eyes and I turned my head away from the screen for a moment. Then I moved the cursor over the red dot in the upper left corner and clicked. The PDF disappeared like cartoon-stretched water sucked down a drain.

If I had been more like my sister Jo, who yearned to have information about her birth mother since she was a young girl and had waited decades for the opportunity to retrieve it, I may have felt a great relief, a catharsis, just to have this document in my possession, even unread.

But I was not Jo and I had not pined for a scintilla of information. What Dad had given me in his neat, handwritten note back in the late 1980s, contented me. In fact, recalling that note and comparing it to the tome now sitting on my computer's desktop, I shook my head and wondered: why had Dad's note almost thirty years earlier failed to spark even the tiniest hint of desire in me to know more? It seemed to have sparked little more than a noncommittal shrug.

Why? My best answer is that I did not need what Dad's note contained. I appreciated it and I kept it along with dozens of other pieces of family correspondence I valued. But if I had been haunted by any "not knowing" about my birth mother prior to Dad's cryptic jottings, certainly I would have acted on it. I did not. I read the note, I digested it, I put it back in its envelope and stored it away. In other words, I forgot about it until Kerry's email sparked the memory of it.

After I clicked the PDF closed and stared at the icon on my desktop, I was struck by the feeling I had in that moment: just give me something simple, something easy to digest. Thirty-three pages? I felt like I was at a closing for a mortgage or I was signing up for an IRA and I did not want to deal with all this *\*#!%\** *paperwork.*

In that instant, I was transported back to Nicolet High School, and I was listening to Jo talk about her plans for starting her search for her birth mother. The task would be arduous, expensive, time-consuming, patience-draining, filled with dead-ends and disappointments. Like scaling a snow-covered mountain in winter. I wondered why she put herself through it. I was the adolescent who saw only the obstacles in front of me but not the rewards that lay in the distance.

I wanted the adoption report now sitting on my computer screen. Yes, I wanted it and I'd gone through the easy-as-pie steps to acquire it and now it was in my hands, so to speak. But I was treating it like lengthy instructions for installing a ceiling fan. My high-school self was yelling into my ear, "It's a huge hassle! It's a huge bother!"

What was going on? The cookie jar of my origins is *right here.* Help yourself! No one will slap your hand.

What was I afraid of?

Nothing. Everything.

## 16

My parents never kept the fact of my adoption from me, but there was a fiction attached to being adopted. A fairytale my parents told me, one I lived with for decades. It was so well known to me that I never thought it was not true. All these years later, I no longer wonder if the story was only for me. Mom and Dad told it for us, for Jo and me. We reinforced the storyline with every word, every glance.

Yet it was not a fiction borne of malice or deceit. This fabrication was a gentle, incomplete story a parent used to explain a difficult concept to a youngster, as I suspect I was when Mom and Dad told me the story about my adoption.

As I grew up, I figured out that I was not the only adopted kid on the planet, so other parents, my thinking went, told their adopted children the same story my parents told me. Jo said Mom and Dad told her the story, too. All adopted kids, I figured, heard their adoptive parents say some version of, "You were picked out. You were chosen."

I accepted Mom and Dad's story without question. But when the adoption report from Wisconsin arrived in my inbox, that story, I realized, was now at stake. I had a comfortable account of my history whose every nuance I knew by heart. And suddenly I was a child again, frightened by the unknown. This new, fat PDF staring at me from a corner of my computer's desktop, waiting for me to click on it again, held a possible alternative version of the story I knew so well, that I'd cherished and retold for years. This PDF icon on my screen seemed to twitch, like a strained muscle, threatening to crush my tidy view of the world.

"Go down this rabbit hole," I heard myself say, "and there's no telling what you'll find. You might not like any of it."

I also heard another voice, gentler, less ominous, yet warning.

"Walk away and you'll regret what you left unlearned."

That was the voice I listened to.

A fter I had closed the PDF the first time on May 25, 2017, I tried to put the adoption report from Wisconsin out of my mind.

About a week after the PDF arrived by email, the hard copy version that Kerry Lenzendorf had promised arrived by mail. I opened it, but let the thick, white manila envelope and its contents sit on my desk for a few days.

It was now early June 2017. It was time. No more delaying. Instead of clicking on the PDF on my desktop, I emptied the envelope of its thirty-odd pages, rapped them against my desk to even them out, and I began.

First, I flipped through the whole thing, keeping the pages in the order in which they were printed. Kerry assembled the document from the records she had uncovered. They slid out of the envelope, I thought, exactly as they were housed for the last sixty years. They should remain that way. They were, after all, a kind of time capsule.

The report included a cover letter from Kerry. These lines stood out:

"As for your birth father, paternity was not legally established meaning he didn't provide any legal testimony or provided (sic)

DNA. WI Law doesn't allow our program to release alleged father information."

The report consisted of sixteen separate documents, most of them official forms. Some were filled in by hand, the rest completed in a typewriter. Some were only half a page in length, others four or five pages, single-spaced, typewritten narratives. A cursory glance revealed acronyms, undefined and mysterious officialese from Wisconsin bureaucrats. Perhaps context would manifest meaning.

I started at the beginning and made my way through the entire report chronologically. I was rewarded on the first page, titled "Family Face Sheet" (that's not a typo — the printed form read "Face"). My birth mother, Irene, and her first husband, Eulo —she called him Junior—were married on November 22, 1952. This was my birth month and day, four years later. What might Irene have been thinking as she went into labor and delivered me thirty-six minutes after midnight on November 22, 1956? It would have been her fourth wedding anniversary to Junior, who had died in a car crash more than a year earlier and who, I had to remind myself, was *not* my birth father. Could she have been aware of this coincidence? The significance of the two events could not have been lost on her.

Page three was the "Child Welfare Social Data Card." Here I learned that Irene had given me a name before officially turning me over to the Department of Child Welfare. I was called "David."

For decades, my curiosity lay dormant. No inner yearning, no deep emotional need existed to budge it. But then when I yielded and overcame my fears that the cherished story of my adoption would be shattered by the contents of the pages in my hand, the cookie jar of information about Irene proved irresistible. All my patience fled, and I gave in to curiosity and adrenaline. Insatiable curiosity, surging adrenaline compelled me to skip ahead, a couple pages at first, then rapidly scanning and speed reading.

Until I reached the last pages of the report and found an ordinary-looking document, another official form with the blanks filled in by typewriter. The form had no name that I could see right away, only these words spaced evenly across the top in all capital letters:

STATE OF WISCONSIN COUNTY COURT MILWAUKEE COUNTY

The form, it turned out, did have a name, in mouse type buried in the lower left corner, which is why I missed it: "Order for Adoption." This form was my favorite for two reasons.

The first was its finality. It was an ordinary form requiring its scribe to roll it into a typewriter and fill in the blanks manually. The document transformed itself from an ordinary piece of paper into a celebratory milestone for me because of what it said, even though the actual adoption had taken place fifteen months earlier. The first word, typed in all caps, read:

DAVID

That was me. Or rather, the name Irene gave me.

The last words, typed in upper and lower case, read:

Howard Frederick Ibach

That was also me. Or rather, the new name I was given officially on the day this document was filled in, when my adoption received court approval. Mom and Dad had been calling me Howie since the nanosecond Mom lifted me into her arms and carried me out of the hospital a year before. They always called me Howie.

The day and date on which this document was completed was the second reason why it was my favorite of all the documents that comprised my adoption report. This time the writing was in someone's hand, not typewritten, its author unknown:

5$^{th}$ day of February 1958.

Coincidentally, it was Dad's thirty-second birthday.

I was born on November 22, 1956, and—what are the correct words?—*handed over* to my adoptive parents on December 19, 1956.

For twenty-seven days I was David.

The definition of the word David, the origin of which is Hebrew, is *beloved*.

Howard is Teutonic for *brave heart* or *guardian of the home*.

What a stunning paradox. How could the woman who gave birth to me and then chose to give me away name me David? If she knew what the name meant, and I have no way of knowing this, did she name me with intention? Is this how she felt about me? Was I her beloved? And isn't it clear that she planned this name long before I was born? Yes—to all those questions. I know this without a spec of evidence.

My new name signified what I needed most for my journey. Dad chose it because he wanted a name that began with "H" to follow Herbert, his father, and his own name, Harold. Howard fit.

It turns out that everyone got what they needed: Irene, my mom and dad, and me. My names fit. Both of them for each of them.

## 18

There are many George Watsons, but the George Watson who set the events in motion on November 5, 1955, near the Jones Dairy outside Nichols, South Carolina, which resulted in my birth more than a year later, likely never learned what his actions did.

One truth became achingly clear as I read my birth mother Irene's story in my adoption report: I saw a change in the trajectory of her life. I felt it. I heard it. I imagined the sounds from the depths of her soul when the news reached her that George Watson killed her husband, Junior. A quick intake of breath, a gasp, a moan, a quiet "No, no, no..." that perhaps grows louder, pleading, begging. A scream of disbelief. Then tears, hands to her face. Sobs.

A slow unraveling of a young woman who, seconds before she received the news, was thinking about anything other than that her husband would die in a car crash.

One minute, a life imagined with a man she loved, the next, a toppled life.

Yet when I pulled back, I realized I was reading an account of events that transpired many months earlier in the life of a woman I never knew, who was now dead and who died decades ago. The transcriber of this tale, the social worker, filtered the emotion through her experience. She did her best, I am sure, to take down Irene's words verbatim, but these accounts would also have been replete with interpretation, inferences, suppositions, maybe tears. The tale, in measurable ways, was once removed.

In other words, *I* had to do some work. If I simply read the words on the page as if I were looking at a form and did not allow them to touch me, to penetrate my consciousness, I would become a passive rider, as I had been on so much of this journey. I did not want this.

I felt a twinge of fear. I was afraid of the unknown. What if some piece of new information in the adoption report induced a crack in my origin story and caused me to doubt what I had believed since I was a child?

I reminded myself that Mom and Dad had instilled in me an identity fortified by daily reminders that they would never give up on me or my siblings. They did this in simple, concrete ways by the things kids take for granted: They read to us, helped with our homework, comforted us when we fell or failed, said "Yes" when we asked for something, said "No" when the ask was unreasonable. Countless, everyday things built the fortress of my certainty that I was already home in the Ibach family.

But I confess that the fear of the unknown, unexpected revelation penetrated my shell. I rested my belief on my lived experience. Although I would have to wait three years before I discovered an acknowledged expert who confirmed what I knew—that in my core I was safe, I was loved and cared for—I also wondered if I was simply rattled by the process of uncovering my history.

I also rested on my faith. And even though as an ardent believer I know that doubt can creep in, I also know that this doubt is there to remind me that vigilance is ever important. So, I mustered the stamina and courage that came with my faith to immerse myself in this new and foreign world of my adoption. It might have been only a thirty-three-page report, but it felt world changing.

And I have another confession: the first two or three times I read the report, I removed myself. I read the words as if they applied to someone else. I took the formulaic nature of the report at face value. It was nothing but forms, sheets of administrative information. I treated what I would later realize was a *story* as only words on a page. I slipped into a comfortable role I was pretty good at: being rational, clinical, dispassionate, like a scientist.

But I was also pretty good at remembering who I am, my true self. I told myself that I had to slow down to absorb these words, to let them sink in, and give them the time and space to emerge and transform from words that described a person into a visible, breathing human being who was my birth mother, with not just skin and bones, but a unique shape, a voice. A heart. As I focused, and I let go of my fears, words arranged themselves to become a living picture of a woman. Irene materialized slowly. Like a pointillist who applies tiny dollops of paint to a canvas that becomes a recognizable shape, I needed to see the small parts first to view the larger picture.

Here was the only written record of Irene's history and explanation of her decision to put me up for adoption, precisely what any adoptee would desire, especially one whose birth mother had died long ago. I wanted to know its contents, Irene's words, thoughts, feelings. I felt afraid, but I didn't allow my fear to rush me. I took my time.

I was beginning to understand the tangle of emotions I had experienced at first when I hesitated to open this document and read its contents. I was wrong about the nature of my fears. I was afraid, but not about any one bit or combination of bits of history that might damage my story. I was beginning to feel a sadness for Irene. Not pity, nothing like pity, but instead a heart-breaking weight of empathy for her draped itself around my shoulders and staggered me. The impossibility of the decision she had to make, that she *had* made, gave me a chill.

I found within these thirty-three pages a dense, single-spaced three-page interview with Irene conducted by a social worker. The interview began on June 13, 1956, in a social worker's office in the Department of Child Welfare and Development. Irene was about three months pregnant. The social worker refers to her by her first husband Eulo's (Junior's) last name—not, I reminded myself, my biological father:

*Mrs. Small is an exceedingly attractive young widow with a great deal of charm. While she is very feminine and petite, she is an intelligent young person who is trying to face a difficult situation bravely.*

The anonymous interviewer misspelled Irene's maiden name, writing Manousas rather than Manousos. Every subsequent reference to it is also misspelled. I double-checked against her obituary and her neat signature on two or three documents in the adoption report. This error escaped my notice the first three times I read the document.

How many times did this writer, or any other social worker, use the phrase *who is trying to face a difficult situation bravely*? Was it an occupational cliché? Did the writer use it by rote?

*Mrs. Small said she had every intention of remaining in the south with her children* (daughters Susan and Jayne, my half-sisters, whom I learned about a week earlier in Kerry Lezendorf's email) *as she had a lovely home and would have had sufficient money to manage on through social security and insurance which her* (late) *husband carried.*

I took a breath: Irene, my birth mother. Her two daughters, Susan and Jayne, also my half-sisters. Her late husband, Junior, who died more than a year before I was born and was therefore not my birth father. I was beginning to feel as if I was in a Russian novel.

And then Irene's veneer cracked a little.

*She said that people were narrow minded about many things and were overly religious* (in Mullins, SC). *She used as an example [...] the fact that most people felt that it was dreadful for a young girl to smoke, and her mother-in-law in particular said it was a high crime. Her mother-in-law, a widow, owns a large tobacco farm and while she raises tobacco for other people to smoke, she does not approve of the use of the weed herself.*

The report continued:

*Mrs. Small said that she found adjusting to living without her husband very difficult and was mixed up and very sad.*

Then we arrived at the crux of the matter.

*A young friend of her (late) husband offered to help her with some of her problems and she accepted his interest in her affairs. She indicated that life in this little town was so dull that she felt it was not wrong to accept invitations from a bona fide friend of her husband. She blames herself severely for what happened as she says she should have known better, and she obviously has a very great feeling of guilt at having become pregnant.*

These sentences were buried near the bottom of the page, and I didn't grasp their significance the first couple times I glanced through the report. But eventually I slowed down and took them in.

"A young friend of her (late) husband..." and "...she accepted his interest..." and "...feeling of guilt at having become pregnant." Who was this *young friend*? It's clear that Irene and the young friend had become close. And within only months of the death of Junior, Irene's late husband.

This young friend was my birth father. Who was he? His identity was not clear.

Five pages into this long, single-spaced narrative, the social worker dropped a new, opaque abbreviation into the story: AF.

## 19

Acronyms, business jargon, insider lingo. But what was AF?

As I read my adoption report, I found myself thinking back to my ad agency days when we met a new client and began the process of learning the business, which required me to decipher strange and unfamiliar nomenclature. I had not read far into my adoption report before I discovered abbreviations and acronyms. They were everywhere:

PGM, PGF, PUs, PAs, TPR, MGM, MGF. Most were easy enough to untangle: PGM—paternal grandmother. PU—paternal uncle. TPR remained an enigma for a long time, and when I learned its definition, I remember feeling a gut punch: termination of parental rights.

And then there was the ubiquitous AF.

I turned AF over in my head. Nothing, aside from the twenty-first century abbreviation for "as fuck" seen often on social media. But this document was written in 1956. It refused to release its Eisenhower-era secret. Sherlock Holmes I was not. I had absolutely no experience with child welfare departments anywhere.

AF? What was AF?

Then I remembered Kerry Lezendorf's cover letter. She told me that the State of Wisconsin does not "release alleged father information."

AF, alleged father. That was it. That had to be it.

And then I read this:

*When* (Irene) *discovered that she was pregnant and told the AF, he wanted to marry her immediately, but she said she felt a forced marriage was just no good and that keeping this child would not be good because she would always have a feeling of guilt about it and she feels that would affect the child and it would be much better off in an adoptive home.*

A single sentence, unwieldy and in desperate need of punctuation, dropped two anvils on my head at once.

The first was that "AF" was the "young friend of her (late) husband" whose interest and attention she thought was "not wrong" to accept. AF: Alleged Father.

*My* father. My birth father.

So now I had new information. I skipped ahead in the report, but this time in search of something specific. AF appeared many more times, but nothing more than the initials *AF*. No name. Wisconsin was mum on this one, by law. So, my discovery proved unhelpful.

The second anvil was stark. The words were clear:

*... keeping this child would not be good because she would always have a feeling of guilt about it and she feels that would affect the child and it would be much better off in an adoptive home.*

This admission was stunning, and I had to read it a few more times before the words' meaning sank in. She would feel guilty and feared her guilt would *make her a poor mother*. And that this guilt would also affect me.

There it was.

A sixty-year-old man, I had scars of my own, a lifetime's worth of joy and loss, triumph and disappointment. In the quiet of my living room, sitting on my sofa, my Calico Jersey curled on my lap, the adoption report in my hands, Irene's words buzzed in my head and my stomach contracted in numbness.

What should I have expected from this collection of papers and forms that arrived first in my inbox and then in my mailbox? Probably not Irene's direct answer. But I wanted to know why I'd been placed for adoption. And my birth mother delivered the answer.

My sister Linda and I have had many talks about this part of my adoption report. As a mother of four children, she had an unsurprisingly biased view.

"She wanted something better for you." She said this to me more than once.

The lawyer in her tried to ferret out the facts. The mother in her was sympathetic to Irene so I did not argue with Linda and remained quiet and uncertain.

"If she would have felt guilty about keeping me, isn't that being selfish?" It was not an accusation but a sincere question because I did not know how to answer.

Linda and I were separated by half a continent and when we spoke, it was usually on the phone. But I could see her in my imagination from years of arguing and bickering when we were growing up, and later, as adults, reveling in circuitous conversations. Her eyes would bore into me, and she'd lean forward to emphasize her point, as if I were on the witness stand and she were cross-examining me.

"But she put *you* ahead of her feelings."

She didn't end with "Right?" but I could hear her tacking on the question. She left it to me to decide.

Was I hurt or was I startled by Irene's answer? Engulfed in emotions was closer to the truth. What was I supposed to feel? Acceptance? Relief? Forgiveness? Anger? Sadness? All of these? None of them?

When the answer arrived, it burst from me in surprise, like a seed pushing its new, green shoots upward out of the ground, testing the unknown space above.

It was not yet ready to be said out loud, but the feeling was real. It was love, a slowing of my heartbeat, a comforting ease in my breathing. Love for my birth mother. Love for a stranger I had never met. Funny how love works. Impossible how love works.

## 20

Irene's story in the adoption report was about waiting. Irene was waiting for me to be born. Waiting for her life to take a new course. I recalled words from the late Howard Thurman, former professor of theology at Howard University, author of more than twenty books on spiritual discovery and inspiration, and mentor to Dr. Martin Luther King, Jr.

"Waiting is a window opening on many landscapes," he wrote in his collection of meditative essays, *For the Inward Journey*. He described four kinds of waiting. My favorite is this: "[Waiting] is the experience of recovering balance when catapulted from one's place."

My birth mother faced a wait of nine months until I was born. She uprooted her life in Mullins, South Carolina, with her two young daughters, Susan and Jayne, and relocated to her mother's house in Milwaukee. There she waited.

And thought about what? She had time to think, to doubt, to perhaps have second thoughts about my fate. Did she consider keeping me? The idea of ending her pregnancy may have crossed her mind, though the prospect of such an endeavor would have been beyond frightening in the 1950s.

Irene, I was learning, was a determined woman. She said no to my birth father's first marriage proposal and had plenty of time to reconsider. She did not. At least not then.

Still, she faced nine months of thinking, probably questioning her decision, no matter what else she did. How did she keep herself occupied? She could have worked. She was a nurse, but I have no indication that she tried to find a nursing position in Milwaukee. My belief is that she worked hard at hiding her emerging condition.

Thurman's perceptive analysis of the unique ways we wait helped me see into Irene's heart, and I think brought me closer to her.

"For some," wrote Thurman, "waiting means the cessation of all activity when energy is gone and exhaustion is all that the heart can manage. It is the long slow panting of the spirit. There is not will to will — 'spent' is the word."

It is not hard to imagine Irene is this place, but only for a moment. She may have given herself permission to be hopeless, but only long enough to gather her bearings. How can I be certain? I cannot. I admit that I've now crossed into speculation, colored by a bias I am acquiring for a woman I never knew. But I am starting to know her. And here I will go out on a limb and say that while she waited to bring me into the world, her waiting was not the wait of the hopeless, the exhausted, the *spent*. This is not the picture I have of her. Or maybe I don't want to see it.

I don't see Irene as exhausted or spent and Thurman showed me why.

"For some," he wrote, "waiting is a time of intense preparation for the next leg of the journey. Here at last comes a moment when forces can be realigned and a new attack upon an old problem can be set in order. Or it may be a time of reassessment of all plans and of checking past failures against present insight. It may be the moment of the long look ahead when the landscape stretches far in many directions and the chance to select one's way among many choices cannot be denied."

I will never know what Irene thought about over the long

months when she carried me. If she shared her thoughts beyond the words taken down by the social worker who completed her official intake documentation that is part of my adoption report, I have not come across them. But there is no doubt in my mind that she peered ahead.

Thurman perfectly describes what I think was Irene's place in the world as my birth date arrived. She was endowed with "the courage to demand that light continue to be light even in the surrounding darkness." Her candle was lit by remembered radiance, a glow she would need to sustain her.

While she waited, I could see as I read the report, she thought about where she would live after I had been born. Would she stay in Milwaukee? Would she return to South Carolina?

Irene unfolded her life story to the social worker who wrote much of the adoption report I read, and I saw how it unraveled. Here she was on June 13, 1956, five months before I arrived:

*Having had two very lovely little daughters, she said that it is going to be a terrific emotional experience to give up a child that you carry for nine months, but she believes she can go through with it and is planning to release. She said all she would want to know (is) if it was a boy or a girl.*

The Intake narrative continues.

*Mrs. Small is hoping to keep the knowledge of her condition from her (late) husband's family as she plans to return to her home in the South after this is over. She explained her absence to her husband's family by saying she wanted a vacation in the North during the summer months, then she may just say that her mother needs her help for awhile* (sic) *longer which will explain her remaining in Milwaukee beyond a vacation period. Since the children are not going to school* (because they are too young) *there need be no questions raised about her lengthy stay in Milwaukee.*

I felt the anxiety in these words. She had to work hard to navigate unsparingly difficult circumstances. As was normally the case, a woman almost entirely had to deal with an unwanted pregnancy on her own, without benefit of financial or emotional support from a partner. Although she had the help of her Milwaukee family, Irene had to dig deeply into her emotional reserves to invent a story to protect her privacy.

*Mrs. Small is a little concerned because she has left her home to be watched over by the AF and she said she had written him twice since she came to Milwaukee and has received no reply from him. ... The thing that does bother [her] now is that she is living in her old home neighborhood, and she believes neighbors are beginning to look at her and wonder why she is in Milwaukee with her mother when she has a home in the South. Her mother would like to have her make an excuse, use a fictitious name, state she made a hasty marriage after her husband's death, and the new husband did not treat the little girls the way he should. ... Mrs. Small said she is not a good liar, and she feels she would just be getting herself more involved. She does plan to give this more thought if it would ease the neighborhood situation for her mother.*

And then a little further in the transcript, I found this:

*Mrs. Small's husband (Junior) was the only boy in a family of seven. His oldest sister had two illegitimate children before she was married so this type of problem is not new to the family.*

A few paragraphs later, the social worker, in a section labeled "Impressions," described Irene as a "very troubled young person who is apparently working out her unusual problem in an intelligent and determined way." Irene was referred to as a "young widow who is illegitimately pregnant and who wishes to TPR."

TPR meant "Termination of Parental Rights."

Admittedly I was stopped cold when I learned the meaning of TPR. Leave it to the bureaucrats, or the lawyers, or both—all of them men, of course—to brew such a phrase. It achieved its desired response: I felt a clammy chill. Even saying the letters out loud, T P R, felt like hitting a wall. Choose this route, they said, and the result is a stark ending.

What this report did not reveal, what it was designed *never* to reveal, was the moment when the reality of a woman's decision to let her child go and give it up for adoption finally registered in her head or in her heart. It did not address how it happened or what she felt at that moment. This was not such a report's purpose. It was not a personal diary. It was not a confessional. It was a factual summary. And it was the epitome of sterile.

Yet this was the only window I had into the life of the woman who bore me. Though I could not bear to read these words closely the first time, now, as I read them, I begged them to shed their surface opacity and show me ... something, anything, that would help me understand Irene.

Irene was not a new mother, which had to have influenced her thinking. I was soon to be her third child. As a widow with two (almost infant) daughters, she had a monumental responsibility. Yet she had grit. She was steely, determined.

Irene was also conflicted. AF, who was still a mystery to me, did not appear out of nowhere. There was more to this story, and it was not apparent in the pages of this report.

But Irene was clearly vulnerable. She did what so many women of this era did when faced with this situation: she returned to family and, fortunately for her, they received her gladly and protected her.

THE NEXT ENTRY by the social worker was dated July 12, 1956, about a month later. Irene has had a change of heart.

*Irene enjoys living in Milwaukee and hates the thought of returning to her home in the South and will return only because it is the home which she and her (late) husband built. She is still quite broken up over her husband's tragic death. She has no financial worries as she receives social security and also* [sic] *expects to receive a settlement from the insurance company for the death of her husband.*

But AF is back in the picture, and he caused palpable stress at home. Whether he wrote on his own or at Irene's prompting is unknown.

*The AF writes to Irene regularly, which is very distressing to*

*Irene's Mo*[ther], *as she would like nothing better than to have the AF put behind bars.*

I had to wonder if Irene ever told her mother that AF, whoever he was, had proposed marriage before she returned to Milwaukee. Her mother did not like her daughter's taste in boyfriends. How ancient is that complaint?

*Irene told her Mo*[ther] *it took two to be responsible for her situation and she was just as much at fault as was the AF, but naturally Irene's Mo*[ther] *thinks her daughter is without any fault.*

How revealing is it that in the same breath that Irene refutes her mother and takes partial responsibility for her situation, she also is not shy about relating her mother's high opinion of her daughter?

THREE AND A HALF MONTHS LATER, October 25, 1956, the social worker wrote up her final thoughts about her meetings "during the past two months" with Irene, who was less than a month from bringing me into the world. What also stood out was another observation about her character, one of many I read throughout this report:

*Irene is surely a very well poised, intelligent person.*

By this point in Irene's countdown, she has decided: she would not return to South Carolina. This was not a surprise, given her state of mind only a few months earlier. Her plans, according to the social worker's report, were to sell her home in Mullins, S.C., and purchase a new home in Milwaukee near her mother. But first she had to return to the South and retrieve her belongings.

These words took me barely a third of the way into my official adoption report. They were followed by terse forms and other paperwork related to my birth and placement in foster care until my adoptive parents took me home.

Like a movie trailer, my adoption report had me hooked, only to be left dangling.

## 21

Irene was dead. AF, the abbreviation for alleged father, was a non-entity, a man without a name or a face. Nowhere in the entire thirty-three pages of my adoption report does his name appear.

Too many questions remained unanswered. My birth mother died at the age of forty-six, but what was the cause of death? Who was my birth father? Since this report had no clues that I could ascertain, how would I uncover his identity? Where were my half-sisters, Susan and Jayne? Were they still alive?

The most bedeviling question, however, was this: where should I go from here? I now had a substantial trove of information about my birth mother and a sliver of background on my birth father. I knew something of my birth mother's immediate family. But between 1956, when I was born, and 1976, when Irene died, sat a cavernous void. I knew nothing about this twenty-year gap. The information in the adoption report ended a little over a year after I went home with my adoptive parents. I had two half-sisters, and their biographies were missing.

Although my adoption report told me nothing about my birth father, Irene testified that the man wanted to marry her and that impressed me. But the genesis of the report in my hands was Irene.

The report began with Irene, and it ended with her. Or rather, me.

If I were to conduct a search in 2017 for whoever constituted my birth family, where would I begin? I began at the end.

---

## 22

I began my search where everyone begins any search in 2017: the Internet.

My computer browser's default search engine is Google, and I started there. I typed in every variation of the surnames listed in the adoption report. Nothing. Nothing that I did not already possess, namely obituaries and photos of graves.

I was at a complete dead end. Not even a crumb.

Then it hit me. The death certificate. Irene died in 1976 at the age of forty-six. She died in South Carolina. A death certificate is a public record. Back to Google, I typed in *"Death certificate South Carolina."*

A website. A few links. There it was. All I had to do was order a copy. Type in relevant information. Pay with a credit card, and wait.

It was a long shot. Perhaps the death certificate would reveal more family information or more details about my half-sisters Susan and Jayne. But I was also curious to discover the cause of Irene's death. My gut reaction told me it was something completely unexpected: a catastrophic accident or cancer.

The wait lasted less than two weeks. When I opened my mailbox one day, I found a nondescript envelope from South

Carolina. Inside was a photocopy of Irene's official death certificate.

Irene died of pneumonia eleven days after suffering a stroke. More specifically, she had had an aneurysm. She had lingered in a coma.

I was no closer to finding her daughters than when I began. So I went back to the adoption report. There it was, hiding in plain sight.

A clue.

## 23

My birth mother's identity and the breadcrumbs even a child could follow to find it, stared me right in the face. Irene married Berlon McCrackin. They were married when she died. Her obituary said so, as did her death certificate. The clue to finding my birth sisters was right in front of me, in black and white as they say in detective novels.

Yet I never put two and two together. Not right away.

In my ignorance, I found another option and at the time it was so compelling I could not ignore it. The clue would have to wait.

My birth mother's maiden name was Manousos. But I had been searching for Susan and Jayne by using what I thought were their current surnames, Junior's surname Small. Kerry Lezendorf made handwritten notes on Junior and Irene's obituaries that came with the adoption report from Wisconsin, including Susan and Jayne's first names and dates of birth, but no surnames. In the absence of any other clue, I drew the conclusion to use Junior's surname, but those searches led nowhere.

Another avenue—I started with Irene's older brother, Ronald Manousos, whose name was also in the adoption report. At the time, this seemed the logical route to pursue.

A website called People Finder promised results: I typed in what I knew, Ronald Manousos, paid with a credit card, and hit enter.

In less than thirty seconds, I had results.

As I scrolled slowly into the interior of the message on my computer screen, the hair on the back of my neck stood up, as if the faded photograph of Irene taken when she was eighteen had whispered something barely audible into my ear: an exact match to the name I had typed in, Ronald Manousos.

An address appeared in Milwaukee, where Irene had once lived.

What I saw next sent a jolt through me and I leaned in closer, trying to focus. A telephone number with an area code I remembered from my childhood: 414.

If he were alive, Ronald would be ninety-one in 2017. Irene died at forty-six, which did not bode well for family members' longevity. It was doubtful Ronald would still be alive. But I had to start somewhere.

The name, address and telephone number were for Ronald. The address was in West Allis, a suburb west of the city of Milwaukee. There was a name next to Ronald's—Karen, age seventy-five. His wife? I hoped so.

Now what?

For the second time in less than two weeks, I hesitated. But I was kidding myself if I thought I could have abandoned my search now.

Looking down at my cell phone, I touched the numbers on the keypad, walked from my desk to the kitchen, leaned against the counter, and stared at the green icon of a telephone glowing back at me.

There I stood, knee-deep in quicksand and I felt myself sinking. This was more than words on a page, facts and figures, official documents, court transcripts. My heart pounded. My breath made a fast retreat out of my lungs. On the other end of this electronic device could be a voice. A human being. What would I say?

I had not rehearsed anything I wanted to say. This was "winging it" by an order of magnitude. This was me operating on impulse, adrenaline, instinct.

It was a Sunday afternoon. June 11, 2017.

Oh hell, why not? I've come this far. I can't stop now.

One sweaty finger pressed the green phone icon. It rang.

No one answered.

But there was an answering machine. Not voice mail, an old-school answering machine. On the machine, I heard a woman's voice, but I did not leave a message.

When my breath returned from its hiding place, and my heart returned from its sprint, a calm settled over me. This call did not get me very far, but I had taken another step.

Not a bad bit of work for the $1.23 People Finder charged me.

## 24

Jo's experience with her search for her birth mother reminded me that I wasn't alone in my indecision about what to do next. Twins often sense each other's feelings, but Jo and I were not twins. We were brother and sister. We were both adopted, from different birth mothers, but there was that *something else* that we shared, an intangible thread—not exactly like twins, not exactly like blood kin—but a psychic connection I believe adoptees understand.

So, I should not have been surprised when I learned that Jo had been having similar doubts about what to do next after she received her adoption report from Wisconsin. She had learned that her birth mother, like mine, had passed away. But her birth mother had lived into her early eighties. Jo also learned that she had five younger half-siblings. One piece of news moved her.

"One of my siblings was adopted," she said. Jo didn't have to say more because I could hear the emotion in her voice, as if her birth mother had reached out through her adoption report and said to Jo, "I couldn't keep you, but I can honor you by adopting someone else's child." I knew Jo treasured that news.

But I was startled nevertheless when Jo told me she decided not to connect with her birth siblings. She knew their names and ages, and where they lived, and that, she said, was enough for her. Instead, she reached out to two of her birth mother's brothers, one who lived only twenty minutes away from Jo in Phoenix, the other who lived in Florida. They spoke on the phone, exchanged emails and texts. Jo even visited the Phoenix birth uncle and his wife.

"I don't need to know more," Jo said to me in a phone call when I pressed her for her reasoning. She had been the one who always talked about finding her birth mother. And that's exactly what she did. We both found our birth mothers.

So I cannot blame Jo for ending her journey when she did. And who can say she won't change her mind one day and take another step.

If Karen was in fact Ronald Manousos's wife, that would make her Irene's sister-in-law. Karen might know some Manousos family history. What I wrote in my journal after the unsuccessful call to Karen reverberated in my head.

"I don't need to make this call," I thought to myself. "I could stop here and be content. Jo is."

That thought sat in my head for about a minute. I couldn't stop. I had to make the call. I had to know more.

The unanswered telephone call to Karen, however, gave me a reprieve. First, I needed to talk to a friend, someone whom I trusted and whose counsel was steadfast. Naturally, I called my sister Linda.

"You could be a complete surprise," she said. "Whoever you talk to, they might not be happy to hear from you."

I agreed.

"Just be prepared," she cautioned. "They might hang up on you."

"Yeah," I said. "Assuming I can even get words out."

She laughed. And then I heard the two words she says whenever she bids someone goodbye, whether you're standing in front of her or speaking on the phone. They may have seemed odd, but coming from Linda, they were reassuring:

"Have fun!"

My thoughts needed settling after my talk with Linda. There were many possible outcomes of a conversation with potential kin of Irene's: I could be an unwelcomed secret now exposed. I had to be prepared for the worst. I had to be prepared for disappointment.

"I am torn now," I wrote in my journal that day, "between pursuing my half sisters, and letting it go. I know I have them—or had them if they aren't still alive—and that may be enough. I will let it sit for now."

My decision was inevitable. Too much momentum pushed me forward. Karen could answer my questions. When I start something, I like to finish it, and I was not nearly finished.

Later that day, Sunday, I called Karen again. The time was 5:41 p.m. in Los Angeles, two hours later in Milwaukee. Speaking in front of sizable groups of people is what I do. The larger the crowd, the more at ease I felt. But sometimes, talking to one person could be unnerving, especially a new acquaintance. Maintaining eye contact was a challenge. A telephone conversation created separation but did not make it easier.

The phone pressed to my ear, I listened to the rings. My heart pressed again my chest *and* crept upward in my throat. Panic redux—two hearts, neither cooperating.

A woman picked up.

"Hello?"

"Hi, hello ..." I said, at least I think that's what I said.

"... Um, my name is Howard Ibach. Is this the Manousos residence?"

"Yes."

"Are you Karen?"

"Yes, I am," she said. Her voice was pleasant and neutral.

"Is there a Raymond there?" My nerves were so frayed, I forgot the name of Irene's brother.

"No..."

"No?"

"No, there was a Ronald. But he died many years ago."

"Oh? Yes, I meant Ronald. Did he have a sister named Irene?"

"Yes, he did."

Why was she being so patient with me? I would have interrupted much earlier and asked who was calling and what did you want.

"Did she die in 1976?"

"I believe so, yes," she replied.

I took the plunge.

"Irene was my mother. She put me up for adoption in 1956..."

Though my exact words are lost to me, what matters is that I spoke out loud, "Irene was my mother."

I waited for her reply.

A pregnant pause is short compared to what greeted me. Then Karen spoke.

"Oh," she said, revealing the first hint of emotion, "we know about you."

I think I exhaled. I'm pretty sure I remained on my feet.

Karen's voice was friendly, almost familiar. Even though that was not possible, it seemed so. Could it be that she had been waiting by her telephone for me to call?

The heart in my chest quieted. The heart in my throat relaxed. Karen and I spoke for a few minutes. She had a surprise for me. More than one, in fact.

## 25

"I am feeling elated, quite the opposite of my mood only hours ago," I wrote in my journal after I spoke to Karen. "I was rather nervous when I placed the call to Milwaukee, not knowing how my news would be received. I was relieved to know that I was not a secret."

Karen was the widow of Ronald, Irene's brother, and she was my second treasure trove. The first was the adoption report itself. Karen was a living repository of information. She practically burst at the seams sharing what she knew, or suspected.

She said she lived in the original Manousos family residence in West Allis, Wisconsin, where my birth mother, Irene, grew up. I understood that attachment to a place.

"This was the house she moved back into when she was pregnant with you," Karen said, "where she waited out the months until you were born."

Irene's mother had asked her oldest son, Ron, to finish the basement into an apartment where Irene could live along with her two daughters, Susan and Jayne, who were no more than toddlers at the time. Ron, for whatever reason, thought Irene was putting on weight. According to Karen, her husband never figured out that his sister was in fact pregnant.

This seems odd, almost comical. How can a thirty-something man be so naive? It would have been easy to say, "It was the 1950s," but clearly, plenty of people were having sex. For one, I was selfishly grateful for all the sex some people were having. Why my late uncle failed to see the obvious is a mystery. Or perhaps he saw exactly what he wanted to see.

Karen was surprisingly nonplussed by my sudden appearance, as if she knew I would call her one of these days. But I was thankful for her warm welcome and the kind assistance she offered. She answered a key question, and then dropped a few surprises I had not expected.

First, she solved the mystery of why I could not find my oldest half-sister, Susan.

"She was adopted," said Karen, "by Berlon."

By Berlon? Berlon McCrackin?

And then a new door opened.

"I think Berlon may be your father," she said.

What?

"Your biological father," she said. "Berlon married Irene. He adopted Susan and Jayne."

*Berlon is my birth father?*

How did I miss this?

In retrospect, it was easy to miss. No one else caught it either. I shared my adoption report with Linda, Jo, Dad, and a couple close friends. I don't know how closely they read it, but I doubt they gave it a "close read" the way I did. And I did not read it closely at first, but only after many speedy skimmings.

You don't know what you don't know. Berlon was Irene's widower after she died in 1976, but there was nothing I could see, nothing obvious, that pointed to Berlon as the mysterious, unnamed "AF" in my adoption report.

Armed with Karen's revelation, however, the pieces fell into place. I would have needed clairvoyance to see it any sooner.

Now I also know why I could not find Susan or Jayne on a

Google search. I had used Irene's first husband, Eulo Small's name, the man everyone called Junior.

This was the clue I could not see, staring me in the face. Irene's obituary. Irene's death certificate. Both listed her surname —McCrackin.

Susan and Jayne had not changed their names. Their names had been changed *for* them, sixty years earlier. Susan and Jayne had been adopted. *Adopted*! By the man Karen told me could possibly be my birth father.

Then the next surprise, one I had never suspected, but in retrospect should have been no surprise at all.

"You also have three brothers," said Karen.

*Brothers?*

"If I'm right about Berlon, they're your full brothers," she said. "After Berlon and Irene were married, they had three more children, all boys."

Tony, John, and Chip.

Time for another long, breathless pause.

Despite these revelations, I put my feelings in check. Do not feel, I told myself. Do not allow doubt, fear, or uncertainty to throw up roadblocks. Mine was a mission. My destination was no longer some far-off horizon. It was right in front of me. Although I could not see it exactly, I knew it was there, I sensed it. Keep going.

After I hung up with Karen, I headed straight to my computer.

There she was, "Susan McCrackin," on my first Google search. She was on LinkedIn.

A name now became a photograph and an occupation and a location on the map.

This was a living person, the daughter of my birth mother, my oldest half-sister.

Another door. Another decision. But this was not a board game, and I was not playing for paper money. One email could deliver a real prize. My head spun as I realized that only weeks earlier, even an hour before as I puzzled through a decision whether to call Karen a second time, I had never considered this path.

But it was Sunday. I would have to wait.

The next morning, Monday, I sent Susan an "invitation to connect" request on LinkedIn at 7:23 a.m. Los Angeles time. My short message said, in part, "I think your mother put me up for adoption." Susan worked in a suburb of Washington, DC. It was June 12, 2017.

She replied at 7:24 a.m. with only "Howard," and nothing else. She was apparently as rattled as I was and likely hit "send" before she knew it. Her second message came a minute later, at 7:25 a.m.

Sixty-one years, seven months, twenty days, six hours, forty-seven minutes after my birth. Plus two minutes more.

*I am so absolutely thrilled to hear from you. I have toyed with the idea of looking for you and am so pleased you have found me. Please, let's talk. I am at work right now and you can call me ... I look forward to hearing from you soon.*

Toyed with the idea of looking for me? She knew?

Susan knew about me. Karen knew about me. The deep, dark secret I feared I was was not deep or dark or, at least for them, even a secret.

The conversation would have to wait. I was about to begin a conference call with a client.

After all these years, a few more minutes hardly mattered.

But I felt a calm breath return, as if I'd finished a long race.

## 26

When Susan said "Hello," I heard a firm voice, confident, with a gentle South Carolina drawl.

"I knew about a baby," she said early in our conversation, "but I didn't even know if it was a boy or a girl."

Irene, her mother, died when Susan was away at college. Some years later, Susan said, she asked her father, Berlon, if the story about a baby was true.

"He said yes," said Susan, "then he told me never to ask him again. I never did."

Berlon confirmed Susan's suspicions and refused to elaborate. Susan told me that Berlon shut the door tightly on the topic. But I drew some conclusions from Berlon's stonewalling. And I did it without a shred of evidence to support them, only deductive reasoning. Berlon wanted the child Irene was carrying because he proposed marriage, and this is verified by Irene in my adoption report. He already knew that Irene had two young daughters, Susan and Jayne, from her marriage to Junior. If Berlon married Irene, he would have acquired an instant family: two young girls and a new baby on the way.

But Irene turned him down in the early months of 1956 and announced that she was moving in with her mother in Milwaukee. She had decided to give up the baby for adoption, again according to the adoption report, but exactly when she arrived at that decision is not made clear in the report. It's possible that Irene returned to Milwaukee without revealing to Berlon her plans to give the baby up. It's possible she did not make the decision until she reached Milwaukee.

The mystery remains unsolved, but it does not matter because I can deduce the rest.

Irene gave birth to me in November 1956, turned me over to child services in Milwaukee, and decided to move permanently back to the city where she grew up. In early 1957, she traveled to South Carolina to sell the home she and Junior had owned and to gather up her belongings for shipment back to Milwaukee, where she hoped to buy a new home near her mother.

But Berlon was waiting and asked her to marry him a second time. She said yes.

What I do not know and will never find out is what Berlon knew about me and how he truly felt about Irene's decision to give me up. My best guess is that Berlon did not like Irene's decision, but whether he learned about it before or after the fact, I think he decided to acquiesce for the sake of a hoped-for relationship. The baby—I—may have been an abstraction to him, probably not even developed enough when Berlon learned about me to have felt me kicking in Irene's stomach. Letting go of a possibility of new life may have been easier than walking away from the woman he loved. And he may have taken the longer view and saw the opportunity to have more children later.

Another outcome of my adoption is that it may have become an immovable obstacle between the newly married couple, the kind of impasse that lasts the duration of a marriage, a point of contention they may have agreed to not discuss.

Why else would Berlon erect a barrier between himself and his oldest daughter? The topic, it seemed to me, was an old wound that had not healed. Or the wound was reopened and festered at Irene's sudden and unexpected death at the age of forty-six, compounding Berlon's grief. When Susan asked him about this mysterious baby, he may have snapped at her and forever closed the door.

But I was not consumed with these speculations on the phone with Susan. That would all come later, in the quiet moments of reflection after I hung up. Susan cascaded through her story, as electrified by adrenaline as I had been the day before when I spoke to Karen. I wondered, and it could be odd to think this, but did Irene sound like her daughter? Could I be hearing an echo of my birth mother right here, right now?

"You have Momma's nose," she said. "I saw your photo on LinkedIn."

I laughed.

"Wait till I send you a photo of Daddy," she added. "You won't believe the likeness."

She asked me if I was still in Los Angeles.

"About five years," I said, "but this is my second time. I came here in 1993 and moved to Minneapolis in 2003."

"You've moved around a lot," she said. It wasn't a question, but a question was there.

"Yep," I said, and listed off the cities, eight in all, including a semester in Paris after grad school.

"Karen said I have brothers."

"Three!" she said, and I could hear joy in her voice. "I already spoke to Tony and Chip. They can't wait to talk to you."

She did not mention John, the middle brother. I wondered why, but I did not ask. I promised to send her a copy of my adoption report right away.

"What about my birth fath—Berlon?" I asked, not quite sure how to talk about him with Susan. "Is he still alive?"

"No," she said. "He passed in 2003."

Berlon had been born the same year as Dad, 1926. He would have been seventy-six or seventy-seven when he died.

A minute or two into our conversation I heard Susan pause,

then muffled choking and a sudden in-rush of air filled my ear. She began to cry.

Less than three months had passed since my sister Jo texted me to say I could request a copy of my adoption records. That report was now in hand, read and re-read and re-read again. The name of my birth mother and now my birth father in hand, so too a copy of Irene's death certificate. And a small library of stories from one family member, Karen Manousos, the widow of Irene's late brother.

Now, sixty-one years later, I was speaking with Susan, my half-sister, a living offspring of my birth mother, on the phone. And she was crying. Crying in happiness. Crying in relief.

Wetness filled my eyes, my throat constricted, and tears spilled down my cheeks, a secret that was not a secret, released and cleansed, free to breathe and speak at last.

This was my one last leap. Here in my Los Angeles apartment, I spoke on the phone with someone who minutes earlier had been only a name in a faded obituary. For the first time in the more than six decades since my birth, I was talking to blood kin. Blood kin I did not know I had.

Later that day, after I ended our first phone call, I sent Susan a copy of the adoption report PDF I had received from the State of Wisconsin, instructing her to distribute it among as many family members as she cared to.

## 27

W hat is the correct terminology? Bloodline? Ancestry? Parentage? I'm not sure. My late dad Harold and my late mother Martha were my parents. They raised me. Mom died almost ten years before I submitted my application to Wisconsin for my adoption report so I cannot say how she might have felt about it, but Dad was completely supportive of both me and Jo.

My DNA comes in part from a family called McCrackin. It's a Scots Irish name, rich in history, reaching back to the Ireland and Scotland of the fifteenth and sixteenth centuries. The first McCrackin émigrés appeared in the United States in the early 1700s, and they settled, so far as I can determine, first in Tennessee, then in the Carolinas.

Some of the earliest McCrackins made their homes in Horry County, South Carolina, which spoons with neighboring Marion County to the south. My branch of the McCrackins has lived in Horry for generations. Visit any cemetery or graveyard and you will likely find McCrackin headstones scattered among the old family names.

Susan told me in that first phone conversation that she is convinced that her adoptive father, Berlon McCrackin, is my birth father. She confirmed Karen's story. When I saw his photo for the first time, I was convinced, too. The photo is old, but you cannot hide family features. I have my birth mother's nose and my birth father's eyes.

And that was the beginning of what I learned. In addition to Susan and Jayne, I had three brothers I had not spoken to yet. My search for my birth mother unearthed a family.

# 28

After Berlon proposed marriage to Irene a *second time*, and after she said yes, Irene stayed in Mullins, eventually moving to the home where she and Berlon raised Susan and Jayne, and then had three more children: Tony, John, and Chip.

I was as much a missing piece to them as they were a missing piece to me. No one saw. Even the key players didn't have it all figured out. Karen Manousos was not certain. Aside from Berlon himself, Susan was the most informed, but even she did not know if I was a boy or a girl. I was an infant and Berlon forbade Susan from asking about me again.

In my life, I've read many mysteries and my preferred approach to these stories is to be a passenger who goes along for the ride. On this outing, with a thirty-three-page story about my birth mother, I admit I was more engaged because I was part of the narrative. But I didn't make any special effort to guess at the ending. Unlike in a mystery, the only person who could wrap up all the elements of my story into a tidy ending was me. There was no omniscient narrator who would reveal the answer on page 298. A phone call to Milwaukee solved the puzzle, a call to my birth mother's sister-in-law, a call I almost chose not to make.

But like a mystery, the story still had a surprise at the end.

"Fate," wrote the late Howard Thurman, "is the raw materials of experience. They come uninvited and often unanticipated. Destiny is what a man does with these raw materials."

Finding my birth mother and my birth father was never a driving force in my life. I was content with the story Mom and Dad had given me. I knew where and with whom I belonged, I knew who I was, I never felt an emptiness, I never felt incomplete. Other adoptees carry these burdens, but I was not one of them.

Yet when you're handed the key to unlock a treasure chest, you have two options: open it and learn, or walk away. That's the same dilemma I faced when I first received my adoption report. For an instant, I hesitated, but only for an instant. Curiosity is a powerful inducement. My choice was easy.

## 29

After decades of being fully content to know only what Dad had presented to me about my birth mother and birth father on a small piece of note paper in the late '80s, I now possessed knowledge that was surprising and delightful. It was like being a kid on Christmas opening presents. But the knowledge was also anti-climactic.

More than the finding of my birth mother and the discovery of my birth family, I took my first steps not toward filling in blanks, because that assumes something was missing. No, my thinking took a different approach. My adopted life had blessed me, and I reconfirmed this truth. I was grateful to Mom and Dad for everything they had given to me. And not only to me, but to Jo and my younger siblings Mike and Linda as well. We had a dream life, not perfect, but set apart from so many others less fortunate. I am not disparaging the McCrackins, but given a choice, I would not have changed stations. I did not like my life. I *loved* my life. I was blessed and I knew it, long before I learned about Irene. Now I was more certain than ever.

What I let go of, I reminded myself, was that only by meeting and reuniting with my birth family would the so-called emptiness abate. I rejected the premise. My life was full. My life has never not been complete. Irene and Berlon, Susan and Jayne, Tony and John and Chip were simply answers welcomed, unexpected gifts. More chapters to a swelling book. Missing biographical details filled themselves in, but I knew my place and purpose long ago.

Yet I remember a feeling of being gripped, as if by a strong hand on my shoulder, the kind of hand a coach lays on you that makes you stop and take notice. The search for a birth mother, I told myself, was supposed to have been Jo's quest, not mine. Well, here I stood. I could easily have stopped, and I would have been content. I continued not because I had to, not because I needed to, but because every step that revealed something new filled me with more gratitude for the life I already had been living. I had a wonderful life, with absolutely no apologies to Frank Capra.

I leaned on that gratitude and as much fortitude as I could muster, because rounding out my biography with McCrackin family details took me to emotional depths I had not plumbed.

Eyes forward, heart awake. *Brave* heart, the meaning of my name.

## 30

The day after I spoke to Susan, in June 2017, she texted me. "How did it feel waking up with a new extended family this morning?"

I had known about the existence of Susan and Jayne since I received my adoption report from Wisconsin in late May. Yet I devoted no time at all conjuring an image for either woman in my imagination, who I figured would be in their sixties, since they were born before me. I already had the 1940s-era photo of Irene from my report and while I strained to see an obvious resemblance, I noticed that I shared the shape of her nose. I'd had plenty of time to use this old photo to help me sketch in my mind the roughest outline of a face for Susan and Jayne, but I never did it. My entire focus had been on trying to locate them.

When Susan sent me a black and white photo of Berlon in his twenties, I saw instantly how I resembled him, especially our eyes. These old photos would have been enough to see something of my new sisters if I had closed my eyes and thought about it. When I saw Susan's photo on her LinkedIn profile page, I knew I'd found my birth family. Susan's high cheekbones, soft smile, and quiet eyes were a grandmotherly version of her mother, my birth mother.

"It feels comforting," I replied to Susan's text. "It's a revelation to see photos of people who look like me."

"I know!" she typed. "Chip said there was no question you were a McCrackin."

Chip McCrackin, the youngest sibling, born in 1964, almost eight years younger than me, had apparently seen my photo on LinkedIn. At fifty-three, Chip was my new "kid" brother. He had been a fire fighter and a police officer before his current work as an independent building contractor. He had a LinkedIn profile with no photograph, and only four connections and no recent postings. He lived in Nichols, South Carolina, and owned a home a mile or two from the family farm where he grew up with his parents, Berlon and Irene, and his siblings.

But I did not indulge in such imaginings about Chip. There was no time to think about his appearance. My new brothers popped into my world on Sunday afternoon, and they learned about me on Monday, the next day. It took me a few weeks to track down Susan, but only hours to make the connection and then speak with her. That's when I learned I had three brothers and started to collect a trickle of information about them. A super sleuth I am not, but my discoveries landed on me like a sudden downpour. The avalanche of information that hit me in the early summer of 2017 startles me still. Yet I took it in with equanimity.

In Susan's eagerness for me to get to know everyone instantly, right this second, she emailed me twice in about three days after we spoke on the telephone. Her missives contained lengthy back-stories on my South Carolina siblings. Her narratives raced past my eyes the way the adoption report from Wisconsin had months earlier: too quickly to grasp the details. But this time, I felt no hesitation about going back for a second and third read, slowing down and taking in the abbreviated biographies. It was as if Susan had invited me into the vestibule of this new home called "McCrackin." The warmth embraced me, and my heart was calm. I had steeled myself for the worst, first from Karen, then from Susan, although I must admit that I wasted no time reaching out to Susan the morning after I acquired her contact information. I did not want to give myself a lot of time to think about Susan's possible reaction. My fears, thankfully, had been overblown.

Susan surprised me with her transparency, as if to say, "Okay, you're family. Here's the good and the bad." She was guiding me from the McCrackin vestibule into the kitchen and inviting me to sit down for coffee. Her combined emails added up to more than two-thousand words and they read like a treatment for a television melodrama.

What's with these McCrackins? First Irene in the adoption report, loquacious about her life in the South, encouraged to speak by her social worker. Then Susan, taking the role of family spokesperson and literally dumping almost a lifetime of experiences about her brothers and sister in a couple of emails. She closed the first one by saying, "I'm running out of steam, but still trying to think of what I need to tell you next." Her fingers must have cramped from all the typing.

She told me quite a story, and although she worried that she was rambling, it came together almost seamlessly. She wrote about marriages gone bad, divorces, children with disabilities, an attempted suicide, illnesses, but also about the remarriages and happy grandchildren, successful jobs, and careers. In other words, the way she described the McCrackin siblings sounded like what my siblings and I had experienced. Not detail for detail, but the mix of heartache and joy that defines families everywhere.

"So welcome to the totally dysfunctional relationships of the McCrackin clan!" she wrote.

Her news was a lot to take in. The difference was, I was reading about living, breathing people. They were alive and well, even if they were on the other side of the country.

In the back of my mind, I wondered if my arrival would be upsetting to someone in South Carolina. After all, I was that guy from Los Angeles who says he's Irene's child that she put up for adoption decades earlier. Someone might doubt. Someone might be rattled by the news.

Those thoughts stayed in the back of my mind. One step at a time. Susan said in one of her emails that she thought Chip had reached out to me already. He hadn't, not yet, but I took her comment as a positive sign.

When you acquire a new family the way I just had, not through marriage but by gaining access to a legally locked box— now unlocked—one that hid family details for legitimate reasons for so many years, I think this is what they call a paradigm shift. Or could it be a waking dream? I maintain that I didn't change, not really, but my perceptions changed.

My mischievous side conjured farfetched scenarios ripped from sci-fi novels. In one, I'd been part of some backward-facing witness protection program, where my past had been hidden to protect me from unruly gangsters, rather than the expected version, where I'd be given a new identity to live out my life in anonymity. In another, I'd awakened from a sixty-year bout of amnesia and now I could remember a past I did not know I had. In a third, I was in an episode of Rod Serling's *The Twilight Zone* and a postal worker delivered an old envelope with a five-cent stamp affixed to it and when I opened it, I discovered a letter from a long-dead relative telling me a family story I could hardly believe, but one that felt right.

These flights of fancy amused me, but I confess to having thought about all of them. And were they flights of fancy? Not entirely.

Something was different, but I was still me and I struggled to put words to the sensation. The best I could come up with, still inadequate, was to have had some valuable item returned decades after misplacing it, like a wallet that sat in a Lost and Found office at the train station since 1956 finally presented to me, dusty, a bit moldy and worn, but intact with its contents unmolested. *But it wasn't my wallet*. It belonged to someone in my family, yet it found its way back to me. How could this be? There it was, sitting in my hands.

This wallet was valuable, not *in*valuable. My life would not be diminished had this wallet never come back to me. No hole had been filled, although new information came into my possession, but I am who I am with it or without it.

It's as if the two-dimensional Irene will in short order become like a book pop-up so that when I turn the page, she will come to life, or as close to life as I will ever experience. And this little miracle will happen—has the *potential* to happen—because Irene's children are alive and knowable. That feeling was tactile, like a little static electricity spark. It had nothing to do with relieving angst and everything to do with the awe of the possible.

The news of my existence may have had a similar effect on my South Carolina family. I was a revelation, a surprise, but the world continued for them as it did for me. One minute, I had a family— my adoptive family—with siblings. The next minute, I had five brand new birth siblings. And who knew how many aunts, uncles, and cousins.

Sharing the discovery with my Austin-based family gave me an unexpected delight. The news reduced some of the smartest, most articulate people I know to monosyllabic exclamations.

"Five?" said Linda.

"Whoa..." said my brother-in-law, Mike.

"Oh..." was all I got from Dad.

"Really!" I heard Jo say, laughing. "Me too!" But all of Jo's five siblings were younger.

My closest friend in Palm Springs guffawed in disbelief. My gym buddies in Hollywood gave me google-eyed stares before they peppered me with questions.

THE FIRST BIRTH-FAMILY member I heard from after Susan was her younger sister Jayne, my half-sister. She emailed me on June 19, expressing her shock at learning the news about me. Unlike Susan, who had left South Carolina and moved to Virginia, Jayne did not stray far from either family or familiar territory. She lived in Mullins, about two miles from Nichols.

Both sisters worked in education, Susan recently retired from the College Board, Jayne a high school guidance counselor.

"I have to say I really don't know where or how to start this email," wrote Jayne, who had been born a little more than a year before me. She was only months old when her father, the man everyone called Junior, was killed by George Watson. "I was more than shocked when Susan called me last week to let me know about you. I can't imagine what it took for you to search out to find the family that you were never allowed to be a part of. I do hope that your life has been one in that you were with a loving family."

The words, "...never allowed to be part of" stopped me, and I decided she may not have intended to reveal this sentiment, that despite her shock at the news, my existence stirred a possessiveness in her.

I responded to Jayne with a photo of me, Jo, and Dad at Dad's ninetieth birthday party in Austin. Jayne wrote back on June 21.

"I will have to tell you that you look a lot like Uncle John Manousos in this picture. He was Mama's younger brother, who passed..."

Two days later, on June 23, she wrote again.

"I just want you to know," said Jayne, "that mama did the RIGHT thing by placing you with a loving, caring family. Mama had her own demons that affected her throughout her life. When she said (in the adoption report interview) the guilt would affect her and the baby, she was very accurate. Maybe later I will be able to explain, in detail, what I am expressing here.

"I can tell you that through my walk with God," she continued, "I have learned to understand and forgive my mother. Your finding us and allowing me to read this (adoption report) information has helped explain many questions I have had all my life."

I had not yet spoken to my full birth brothers Tony or John or Chip, but I knew that would come.

Thinking about my conversation with Susan, and re-reading

Jayne's emails, I understood in an odd, hallucinatory way what Copernicus must have felt like when, after gazing through his primitive telescope, he concluded that the Earth was in fact not the center of the solar system, but only one of many planets, and that the sun deserved the central role. Everything changed, he realized, but nothing changed.

I had not changed, but I was no longer the same. I did not feel relief, but I had to admit I was touched by moments of deep joy. An arduous journey had not ended. Rather, a door had opened, and I had stepped through. The path led me here and I was proud of myself. My curiosity had been hibernating and now it was awake.

Not so long ago I had wrestled with what Nancy Verrier called "the trauma of adoption" and accepted the basic premise that I, like all other adoptees who were placed when we were newborns, experienced a psychic wound. Some, like me, were not deeply affected and we moved on, while others did not.

But what about my birth siblings? They lived with my birth mother, Irene, who was clearly affected by her decision to give me up. She was probably traumatized by the experience. How did it affect her as a woman? As a mother? As a wife? And how did her decision affect her children? The fact remained that Irene's life changed after me. And it is not an unreasonable assumption to say that the trauma Irene felt rubbed shoulders with Susan, Jayne, Tony, John, and Chip. And Berlon, too. I will never know the answer to those questions, and no one, living or dead, can know the answers either. It is not possible to know because there wasn't a second McCrackin family, one where I grew up with all my birth siblings along with Irene and Berlon—what scientists would call a "control" group they could study to witness any differences.

I did not suffer the trauma Verrier claimed for all adoptees, but I cannot say the same for the lives of my birth siblings. I do not believe they will ever know.

## 31

S usan and I saw each other for the first time on a video call on the Fourth of July in 2017. We were happy, even a little giddy, to finally see each other. We were separated by the entire continent and sixty-one years.

The moving image of Susan on my computer screen was much like the photograph of her on her LinkedIn profile except that she was more animated than I expected. Her cherub-like cheeks charmed me even more on video. Susan smiled as often as she breathed. She was elfish. The young Irene from her 1940s black-and-white photo emerged in Susan's face.

"Hi!"

"Hello!"

"Nice to finally see you!"

"You too. How are you?"

Despite my journal, some of my memories of our first video call were lost, due, I'm certain, to nerves. It was just a video call, but it was so much more than a video call. How much did Susan remember? What stood out for me was not what we said, but that we simply reveled in each other's video presence.

In that moment, I spoke to and beheld *genetic family*. That was a first for me. In my journal, I wrote:

*We talked for over two hours. It was thrilling, emotional,* wonderful! *I now have phone numbers for Chip and Tony, a bit more background on John, the middle brother, and some details about Daddy Berlon.*

The term "Daddy Berlon" was my invention. Susan and my new siblings called him Daddy, but I needed some way to distinguish between my dad and their dad. So, Berlon became Daddy Berlon, although most of the time I called him Berlon, whether I was speaking to my family, my friends or one of my McCrackin siblings or relatives.

I drew a clear line between my family and the McCrackins. My family was Harold, Martha, Jo, Mike, and Linda. The McCrackins were my blood kin, and I felt an instant liking toward them even with only a few texts and phone calls. I wanted to know them better and I wanted to feel connected to them in some way which I knew was nascent in these early days. But I also believed a bond was possible, if only because I wanted one.

Six decades as an Ibach made me who I am. Meeting the McCrackins would not change that, but it could, and I hoped it would help me to see myself through a new lens. As a spiritual person, my priority has always been self-realization. If my new siblings could enable me to see myself differently, in a way that would nudge me to grow, to become a better version of myself, that prospect was thrilling.

Few words that Susan and I shared stayed with me—I was clearly more nervous than I realized—but I remembered that impression. It wasn't clear at the time, but I now know the feeling I experienced was pride of accomplishment: I had done this looming, scary thing that I had challenged myself to do. My goal was to discover family identities and I did it. Now I was looking at my older half-sister, Irene's first child, someone who knew my birth mother. As I sat back in my chair I said, "Cool."

If I had been one of the "maladjusted" adoptees I'd read about in that online discussion forum, my feelings would probably be different. How, exactly, I am not able to say and what would be the point of speculating?

My curiosity was asleep for a long time because I did not "need" to have this information about my birth family. Now that the information was in my lap, my perspective changed. Needing something felt like an addiction, a craving. But wanting something put a different spin on it, like there was a blessing in store.

I have always been a curious person, but now my curiosity felt fresh, alive, like a beautiful breathing creature within me. So, I embraced it. More than that, I was now egging it on. I was rewarded for my decision with blessings I could not have imagined.

## 32

When I pulled out my iPhone and dug into my text strings from summer 2017, I was puzzled to find that I let almost a month pass between my chat with Susan and my first text to Chip. I spoke to Susan on June 12 and texted Chip on July 7. My first phone conversation with Chip took place the next day, July 8.

Why had I waited so long? There were many reasons, and I did not grasp them right away. Jo's decision not to reach out to her siblings reminded me that I could do the same thing. There was no obligation to go further, nor were there any parameters on my search. In earlier stages of this train ride, I was content to be a passenger and trust the engineer to know where she was going. But I took many decisive steps up to this point, and I was too far along now to believe I was a passive rider. I was driving.

But I am embarrassed to say that I allowed some of my friends and acquaintances in Los Angeles to prick me with their daggers. Their comments sometimes brought me up short and contributed to my hesitancy to call Chip.

"They live in South Carolina?" said a gym acquaintance named Derek as he set the weights for the triceps machine he was using. "They're Trump lovers."

"Yeah," I said, "maybe they are. What does it matter?"

Derek, a successful commercial and movie producer whom I'd known for a few years, glowered at me.

"They're family," I added before he could say anything more. "That changes things."

"You don't even know them," he retorted, turning away from me as he yanked the textured metal bar forcefully toward the floor.

"Exactly," I said. "I prefer not to draw conclusions. Why did you?"

Many of my acquaintances at the gym were progressives and in Los Angeles that is almost a fact of life. My producer friend's less-than-veiled sentiment was among the gentler comments I heard. The stereotyping and biases were ripe and revealed people's own prejudices, and I did my best to let them slide. But I could not un-hear what they said.

One more thought pervaded my brain as I let the days drift by before I finally called Chip. There was an inevitability to that telephone call, but my hesitation gave me time to remember the trepidation I felt before I finally read my adoption report. I knew some of my gym buddies were probably right about the political leanings of my birth siblings, but I don't recall ever reconsidering the option to connect with any one of them because they lived in a so-called red state. I concede that I've had heated political discussions with family and friends dating back to my high school years, but I have never allowed a political disagreement to end a friendship or a family relationship. That possibility did not concern me.

But I felt anxious that our other differences might be hard to bridge. Like class issues. Snippets of Susan's emails stuck with me, that none of her brothers attended college. I also remembered hearing her say in the first minutes of our first phone call that she saw right away on my LinkedIn profile that I'd attended Brown University.

"I always thought you'd get a good education," she said. Susan knew more about adoption than she let on because I dug around and discovered that adoptees often move up in the world because placing agencies scrutinize potential future parents and homes.

And there was the other Hindenburg-sized stereotype waiting to erupt: I'm the lost brother who lives in La La Land...er...Los Angeles. My new siblings may have assumed as many incorrect conclusions about me as my gym acquaintances had about them.

These little and not-so-little differences weighed on me.

The decision to call Chip took about three weeks. The fact that I'd already talked to Susan and emailed her a copy of my PDF adoption report probably precluded my disappearance.

Susan was the first blood relative I'd ever spoken to, but she was my half-sister. Irene was her mother and mine, but Berlon was my birth father and she had been adopted by Berlon. These facts were remarkable things all by themselves. Chip was my full brother. He had been born to Irene and Berlon and so had I.

Most of the details of my first conversation with Chip on July 8, 2017, are fuzzy now. I was a little scared, a lot nervous, not sure of what I'd say and for someone who talks for a living, that prospect tightens up the vocal cords. And other anatomical locales. But I will never forget his first words:

"I can hardly believe it," he said.

Chip's disbelief was laced with happy, welcoming surprise, and I could hear it in his voice. Right away, with those first words, I felt more confirmation that the embrace I had felt after speaking with Susan was genuinely felt by Chip as well. Without a moment's hesitation, both McCrackins spoke to me openly, without an ounce of mistrust or doubt. I should have been flabbergasted, and it's possible I was, but Chip and I were too caught up in the moment, just as Susan and I had been a few weeks earlier. Two McCrackins reduced me to a bowl of soft noodles, causing me to fear the worst about talking to them. And then all my uncertainty and fear vanished, as if they were debris weighing on my shoulders and first Susan's, then Chip's hand brushed them away.

Chip's soft, lilting drawl had a calming effect on me. His

South Carolina dialect was more pronounced than Susan's, who'd been living in Virginia for many years, which I think flattened the melody of her speech. On that first call I heard a warmth in Chip's voice that I had not expected. Unbidden, Chip shared with me a personal experience I am not certain I would have revealed so soon in a new relationship.

"I have no memory of Momma," he said, when our conversation turned to Irene and Berlon. His voice was even, with no hint of self-pity.

It would be a familiar refrain, and I was touched to be privy to a deep pain he had carried for decades. I pieced together the details about the day Irene died from Chip and Susan before I met them.

Chip claimed that he remembered very little, almost nothing, about the day, August 12, 1976. This was the date he found his mother, Irene, my birth mother, on the floor of the family home, unconscious.

Chip was eleven years old when he came into the living room, knelt, and reached out to his mother, unconscious, her breathing shallow. He was not accustomed to seeing her lying on the floor, as if she were asleep, dressed in her white nurse's uniform, stockings, white shoes. Had she been in her bed, only a few paces from this spot, he might not have been alarmed. Had her eyes been open, his world would not have begun closing in around him.

But she was prone. She was not in her bed. She was not alert. She was not looking up at him.

Chip knew something was amiss. He didn't know what.

He remembered that he tried to scream for help. The scream didn't escape his lips until enough air penetrated his lungs and he found his voice.

Then the madness began. Others, who had been outside on a hot, muggy summer day in South Carolina, rushed to Chip and their mom. There was chaos, tears. A call to an ambulance.

Chip's memory faded, and I understood why.

Irene had suffered a stroke caused by an aneurysm. She fell into a coma and developed pneumonia about a week later, an inexorable descent. Eleven days after she collapsed, on August 23, 1976, a call came to the house. Berlon answered. Chip remembered the call.

"We were in the living room," he said. "Watching an episode of M.A.S.H."

Irene died in the ICU she had worked so hard to build in the hospital where she was employed, among colleagues who were shattered because they were unable to save her.

Irene was forty-six years old. Anyone would have said she had died too young. Just ask Chip, who was eleven, John who was twelve, Tony fifteen, Jayne twenty, Susan twenty-two, Berlon fifty.

Chip will never forget, and he remembered nothing.


CHIP TOOK me right into the deep-end of his life, as if he were saving up his stories for this call, and I was happily surprised at how quickly we were getting to know each other in that first forty-five-minute conversation. I called him again, not often, but regularly. He texted occasionally, usually with photos of sunsets over the pond he had built on his property.

Twenty-four hours after speaking with Chip, I texted Tony, the oldest of my three younger McCrackin brothers. Susan's McCrackin-family tome of an email—the first one she sent—had informed me that Tony owned a cabinet-making studio, and I immediately drew the conclusion that he probably had an artistic streak in him.

"Hi Tony!" I wrote, "It's Howard, your LA brother. Would you like to speak on the phone and get acquainted? I can't wait to meet you."

Tony replied right away.

"You bet," he wrote. "Same here. Got so many stories about Daddy I want to tell u."

He asked that I call him right away.

"...I am riding with the wife down I-95 about an hour from home."

For the next fifteen minutes, my ear was filled with a deeper version of South Carolina drawl than Chip's. Tony sang and played the guitar and the banjo, and I figured he was probably a baritone, but his speaking voice slid into the lower range of a tenor, higher when he laughed, animated by the smile he always seemed to wear in his voice and his eyes. In recalling our first phone conversation, I could hear this smile even in my memory. Most things he wanted to tell me unraveled as a story, told at a pace that he never changed. Listen or don't, but he wouldn't speed up even if we were walking out the door. I did not ask anything about Berlon during our first phone conversation.

Tony sat in the passenger seat while his wife, Marianne, drove. Marianne was Tony's second wife, but they had known each other a long time. He was her second husband. They were in a late-model Ford Mustang convertible, but I could tell the top was up because I heard no wind or traffic through the phone.

As an adult, I had lived in populous cities and traveled overseas, so I was accustomed to hearing different accents and American dialects. I was practiced at distinguishing between a New Zealander, an Aussie, and a Brit, or a Mexican's Spanish and a Spaniard's Spanish. The Yankee-Southern accent of a Floridian and the slow slushy twang of a Texan were also familiar. A South Carolina dialect was new to my ear and the musicality of the intonations rose on a scale from the flatter singsong of Susan's northern Virginia-influenced patois to Tony's swampy, Bible-Belt syrup. Marianne was busy behind the wheel and did not take the phone, but Tony put it on speaker and held it up to her so she could say hello.

"Naz ta me chew," she said. Her syrup was more like molasses.

What a delight. The strange-but-not-so-strange sounds I heard over the telephone did not put me off. My northern Midwest cadence probably had a similar effect on Susan, Chip, Tony, and Marianne.

The contrast between Nichols, South Carolina, a place I had

never visited, and my adopted home of Los Angeles could hardly be starker. That's the way it seemed to me.

My new family lived in the Deep South. I lived in a place lots of people described pejoratively as the Land of Fruits and Nuts. I faced a gap of experience unlike anything I have ever tried to bridge. Familiar but uncomfortable thoughts crept into my thinking: Was I guilty of believing the stereotype that everyone in the South was a bigot, a racist, a white supremacist? That of course my birth family was one of *them*? My gym buddies had crossed that line in their thinking, or so the evidence seemed to indicate, even if they might have denied it. Had I?

In my life I have been many things: a son, a brother, a friend, a camp counselor, a boss, a mentor, an employee, as well as a lover, a fiancé. How would I do this—be the unknown brother now found?

## 33

The sounds of Susan's voice rang in my head. And three words that played as if on a loop: the Deep South.

My feelings swirled in the first weeks and months as I digested the news of discovering my birth family. My emotional pendulum swung back and forth between excited vertigo and passivity, almost indifference, trying to find some equilibrium.

And then one July day, in a phone call a month after I was breaking in this new pair of shoes called "older half-sister," Susan told me a story that was charming in its honesty, but also alarming. Alarming in the sense that my equilibrium-seeking pendulum came to an abrupt stop. It almost fell off its supporting hook. What Susan told me forced me to awaken to a reality about my birth family that I hadn't thought through.

In high school, Susan told me, she, her younger sister Jayne, and a male friend, tried to steal a wooden cross.

My relief was immediate because she had said "steal" and not "burn." But I also found myself confronting a personal bias: had I expected her to say "burn"?

These words turned over in my head. Susan and I had spoken over the weekend, and I had listened to her in rapt silence, doing my best to reserve judgment, to let her story unfold. Why she was sharing such a personal slice of her past perplexed me, but I chose to stay quiet.

She was recalling a story from her high school days, in the early 1970s. There it was, she told me, lying flat in the yard in front of the single-wide mobile home, in broad daylight. A cross, ready for burning.

"Klan members were our neighbors," she said matter-of-factly. "Some were deacons in the church."

The cross was made of two logs tied and nailed together, eight or ten feet in height, as Susan described it. Nothing special, but even in its prone state, on a hot summer afternoon in 1972, it carried the weight of its own symbolism.

The three high schoolers—my two half-sisters and a boy they were friends with, in a pickup truck—drove by the single-wide.

"Wait, stop!" said Jayne, a sophomore in high school. "Is that what I think it is?"

Susan, a senior, was driving. She slowed, then stopped in the middle of the two-lane road. The only sound they heard was the insistent chug of the engine. The boy, Jimmy, was in back, leaning against the pickup's cab window. He knocked on the glass.

"What y'all stopping for?" he said, his voice muffled by the window.

"Over there," said Jayne, pointing out her window at the object lying in the yard.

Jimmy was a husky fellow, Susan told me, a solid six-two, short-cropped hair, handsome. He turned his gaze.

"Damn," he said.

"Let's get it," said Susan.

Jayne, sitting shotgun, snapped her head toward her older sibling, her mouth agape.

"What?" she said.

"What?" said Jimmy, not understanding the conversation in the cab. "Say again?"

"Just what I said," replied Susan. "Let's steal it. Put it in the back and get the hell outta here."

"What are you two goin' on about?" he said.

"We're gonna steal that cross," Susan said to Jimmy, who'd stuck his head into the driver-side window, his face was now inches from her own.

"She's crazy," said Jayne. "We're gonna get shot."

"Shot is right," said Jimmy.

"No we won't," said Susan. "Jimmy, you get the cross and Jayne and I'll open the tailgate. Hurry before they see us."

"I'm not ..."

"*Hurry!* Do it now!" Susan half yelled, half whispered, pushing her door open and forcing Jimmy back into the pickup bed. He shook his head but knew there was no use arguing with Susan when her mind was made up. He leapt over the truck's side and ran into the yard, trying his best to crouch his six-foot-two-inch frame.

As Susan recalled those events when she and her sister were teenagers, I was forced to wake up and face an unspoken possibility about my new birth relatives: a family history in South Carolina dating to the 1700s meant somewhere in the McCrackin genealogy someone may have owned enslaved people. Or if no one owned them, neighbors, friends, and other family members did. The facts of slavery would have been ubiquitous, unavoidable. Not merely across generations, but over centuries.

I had not asked Susan or any of my new siblings about this issue or their attitudes about race or racism. It would have been rude, presumptuous, condescending, unnecessarily judgmental. And simply way too soon in a new relationship.

But Susan had cracked open the door. She continued with her Klan encounter:

Jimmy never got more than a few feet in the pickup's direction, wood cross in his grip dragging behind him. A dog inside the single-wide started barking and two or three men ran out the door.

They all heard the unmistakable report of a shotgun. Then another.

Instinctively, Jimmy, Susan, and Jayne ducked.

"Warning shots," said Susan, chuckling as she regaled me with her tale.

How the hell does anyone know the difference between a warning shot and one aimed right at you? If you weren't hit that was one possible clue, but I wouldn't bet my life on it.

Jimmy had been dragging the cross in his cupped hands, cross-piece nearest him, backward toward the road, Susan said. On hearing the shots, he dropped it as if it were already burning and ran in the opposite direction, toward the cover of some tall, dense pine. Susan and Jayne scrambled back into the pickup and sped away. But they weren't alone. The Klan members pursued them in their own pickup.

"They followed us for a mile or two," she told me, "until they caught up. When they saw it was us, they dropped back and turned around."

"They knew you?" I asked.

"Oh, yeah," she said. "We knew them, too. But I guess they weren't bothered by us."

Nichols is a hamlet, smaller than a small town. Everyone knows everyone.

"We got quite a yelling at from Daddy," she said, after returning home and telling Berlon what had happened. "But later that night, Jayne and I snuck out and watched them burn that cross."

"You weren't afraid you'd be recognized?"

"No," she said, "but we sat way back from everyone else."

"Wait a sec," I interjected. "What would you have done with the cross if you'd actually stolen it?"

Susan laughed. "I have no idea," she said. "There wasn't much to do for fun. It was kinda on impulse."

"And what happened to Jimmy?"

"Oh, he made it back home," she said. "But he wasn't too happy with us."

Credit to Susan and Jayne for showing some spine, but I

wondered why, after their attempts to steal the cross, they ended up attending the event their actions were designed to prevent. But I sensed no animus, no malice in either her voice or her story. And I would never hold anyone to something they said or did forty-five years earlier.

But I also wondered if regaling me with this high-school adventure wasn't a way for Susan to demonstrate her and her sister's enlightenment to the new Yankee brother from arguably the bluest state in the Union. In the 1970s, they walked a fine line between their social obligations of being neighborly with the people they knew to be Klan and their youthful desire to be, at least in the way their story illustrated it, independent.

When I worked up the courage to ask the indelicate question if Susan knew whether anyone in the McCrackin family, or its many in-laws, had ever owned an enslaved person, I was relieved that she was not offended. I apologized anyway. And frankly, she gave me the answer I expected.

"I never heard anything about slaves in the family," she said. "And the truth was, the family was dirt poor. They couldn't have afforded slaves."

My head was spinning, but one thing was clear: we were family, we were Americans, but our world views would likely be vastly divergent. As they and I had not even met, the path had not yet emerged for me to know how or where to tread.

## 34

The experience of acquainting myself with a new family felt like pulling down an old and unread novel from a dusty bookshelf and beginning to learn the names and backgrounds of the characters, trying to see the landscape where it all takes place. This story was part mystery, part romance, part history, part drama with not quite a cast of thousands. Dozens, yes, because the McCrackin family had been in South Carolina for generations.

Even though I was not a main character in this historical novel, the story belonged to me. It was about me, not directly, but I was part of it. There was something else bubbling up in my consciousness that I had not considered: Would I see my world differently through my birth siblings' eyes? What would they reflect back to me? What could they teach me? Not only about my long-deceased birth parents, but about my life once removed from theirs? There were differences between nurture and nature, and I wondered how much of nature kept its sticky tendrils attached to me. And if even a few of their spirals held on, how would I recognize them? Or would my siblings see them for me?

These were questions I never asked. Until now. And I felt a relief that came with freely asking these questions. My new siblings were eager to share their family stories. I was ready to immerse myself in McCrackin family baggage—all of it. The difference I believed would be significant. I wanted to hear and feel and see what, if anything, we did or said that was alike, the "nature" part of the question, the ingrained, genetic intricacies that siblings have in common. And how did I stand out as unique, different, the "nurture" part of the question, where my adoptive family and my life in Wisconsin affected me? The surface stuff was easy: my Midwest dialect was worlds apart from the South Carolina twang I heard when my siblings spoke. The subtle, unconscious stuff would be harder to distinguish and unpack, at least in the early days. I didn't know what to expect.

Susan and Jayne are my half-sisters, facts I have already shared but for clarity's sake are worth revisiting. Tony, John, and Chip are my full brothers, all younger. I was born between the sisters and the brothers. Tony, John, and Chip are half-brothers to Susan and Jayne.

The stories began with the sibling I met first. They tumbled out of Susan, about her life and growing up in Nichols, South Carolina, which arrived first in emails and texts, then in phone and video calls. These anecdotes revealed a girl and a young woman, indeed an entire family, with mischievous and spirited appetites. Susan revealed more about Berlon, the most mysterious character in this unfolding story.

"Daddy was a farmer," Susan told me, but it turned out that he'd tried his hand at different kinds of farming over the years. And he had inherited the farm and the family home and other buildings from his father, John Mayo McCrackin, whom everyone called "Mayo." Mayo built the family house in 1935, which is where Tony and his wife Marianne now live.

Berlon started out with what I learned were called "cash crops": tobacco, cotton, and corn. South Carolina is tobacco and cotton country, something even I knew. But according to Susan, he quickly realized the limitations of making a living with these crops and converted the farm to feed pigs.

"In time," said Susan, "Daddy also started a feed mill."

It took me a minute, but I realized that "feed" was not a verb but an adjective. So, Berlon was not in the business of feeding pigs but of raising feed pigs, although to accomplish the latter he had to do the former.

When she was a senior in high school, Susan raised her own pigs to help pay her way through college. Her father gave her a pig pen he was not using.

"I'd go to the bank and borrow money to buy pigs," she said. "I would take care of my pigs and all of Daddy's." Her pen held 150 pigs, she recalled. At the end of the summer, she would sell off her lot, as well as Berlon's. Part of her proceeds would pay off the bank loan and the rest she used to pay for her education.

As I listened to Susan tell the story of her family's beginnings, I was fascinated at how different my life had been from the people who were my new relatives. There was no escaping the vast gap in experience and advantages I had lived by comparison.

And then Susan turned a page in her family biography, and I was unprepared for the revelation. At first, I was appalled to learn about a part of Berlon's past, but I quickly got over that and found myself intrigued and spellbound.

When Berlon was in his late teens, he began to hone a bad-boy reputation that he polished for many years. Berlon and violence, Susan said, were intimate partners well known to friends, family, and neighbors. Local police were also aware, even if they had had no justification to confront him about it. Yet.

Susan said that Berlon had a passion for knives.

"Daddy loved a switchblade," she said. "And he had a short temper."

From teenhood until the time he met Irene, in his late twenties, I learned, Berlon was wild.

"He was a fighter," said Susan. "He knew how to use that switchblade."

One or two others in Mullins and Nichols and thereabouts found out, too. The hard way.

Susan told me she cracked up when she read in my adoption report that Irene described Berlon with "broad shoulders." That, she concluded, was Irene's embellishment.

"He was skinny as a rail," said Susan, "and no broad shoulders."

Berlon stood five-foot-eight, according to the social worker's interview with Irene in the adoption report.

"More like five-six," said Susan.

As a young man of middling size and build, Berlon liked to fight. He displayed no fear and seemed indifferent to what others thought about him. Who needed size when he had the psychological equivalent of a roll of dimes balled up in his fists? His handiness with a switchblade would sooner or later draw blood. These were the sharp-edged components of a deserved reputation.

Susan recalled one example of Berlon's aggressiveness, a story pieced together with bits from her brothers and from Berlon himself. A young man she called Roy (she didn't remember his name) had parked his truck along the side of a two-lane road not far from Nichols.

"This was in the early 1940s," said Susan. "Daddy would have been about seventeen."

Roy was killing time. A cigarette burned in his right hand. The heel of his leather shoe was wedged on the chrome bumper of his truck as he leaned against the front hood and smoked.

Berlon slowed his car to a crawl when he noticed Roy's truck on the shoulder. He recognized the young man, smoking. Berlon pulled off the road just in front of Roy, parked, then stepped out and closed his door.

"Beautiful mornin'," he said, "ain't it?"

Roy said nothing.

"You waiting for someone?"

The young man remained silent, smoking, and flicking ash to the ground as if he were alone and no one was watching.

"You listening?" Berlon's throat tightened, his voice rose a note.

Berlon walked slowly toward the truck, in Roy's direction. Sensing something was not right, Roy slid off the hood.

As if an invisible movie director had yelled, "Action!" the two boys prepared for a fight. They tensed. They stared. They drew knives. They spat vitriol. They bled. Berlon cut himself by mistake and he also cut Roy deeply. Roy barely survived. Berlon fled.

Word spread. A reputation was born. Berlon cast his dye in red.

What provoked Berlon? Who knows. It is possible he had no idea either.

Susan seemed entirely at ease sharing this story about a young Berlon. As if she were merely a reporter recalling the facts, with no embarrassment, no regret. After the initial shock, I warmed to the story and found it revealing, foreign from anything I had known, disconcerting in the way you might feel if you found out your best friend was missing a toe.

When I was about the same age as Berlon, I carried a swelling anger toward a high-school classmate, a boy named Charlie, for whom I had an intense sexual crush, about a year before I admitted to myself that I was gay. He humiliated me after I came out to him in my innocence and naivete. I barely contained my rage, but that was the difference between me and Berlon. He had not contained his anger, and I had.

SUSAN TOLD ME MORE STORIES. She loved horses. Her first horse was named Country Boss Squire. Country Squire like the Ford station wagon with the swing-out rear door. Boss, she said, because he could be headstrong. Boss was a steady mount. He was half American quarter horse, half Tennessee Walker. During high school, Susan fell from Boss when they attempted to jump a fence one day. Susan was game, but Boss had his own plan. He balked and Susan flew sideways from her saddle and hit the fence post. She broke her left arm. Irene came running from the house in her pink housecoat and bare feet. Susan, the injured party, remained calm. Irene did not.

"Did you break your arm?" she cried.

"Yes ma'am," said Susan, sitting up and holding her aching limb.

"Oh, no," exclaimed Irene. "Now you won't be able to play the organ!"

Irene was an emergency room-trained nurse who worked at the local hospital, but in that moment she was, in Susan's estimation, not the poised caregiver she had known all her life. Once Susan and mother arrived at the hospital, ER nurse Irene McCrackin was all business and professional again.

When Irene was about six, Susan told me, she earned a nickname.

"Everyone called her Butch," she said.

No one called her anything else. It's a name she acquired in Milwaukee when a neighbor spotted her climbing a tree with her friends. He called her butch, as in a tomboy, a masculine girl, and it stuck.

She may have been a northern girl, but life in South Carolina touched her in subtle ways. Susan said her mother didn't have a Southern accent, but she picked up Southern phrases, bits and pieces of local colloquialisms. Susan, who was about twenty-two when Irene died in 1976, still hears her mother's voice in her head.

"She had a singsong quality to her speaking," said Susan. "Like Meryl Streep when she spoke in her everyday voice." At that point, Susan broke into a song she heard her mother sing when she was a girl.

"I love you a bushel and a peck and a bushel and a peck and a hug around the neck ..."

While Irene and Berlon were both musical, Berlon was the musician. He played banjo and guitar. But Irene could sing, and she could also harmonize. Many nights at home, after dinner, Susan said that Berlon would bring out his guitar. As Irene cleaned up, she'd put on a pot of coffee and Berlon filled the house with familiar chords.

"I can still hear them singing 'That Old Rugged Cross,'" said Susan. "Daddy would sing, and Momma would join him in harmony."

When I dug up the lyrics, I recognized them immediately. And I could almost hear Berlon and Irene singing together.

*On a hill far away stood an old rugged cross*
*The emblem of suffering and shame*

"We'd sit at the table and just listen," said Susan. "We'd try to join in. I can't sing for my life. But those lyrics, I'll never forget them."

*And I love that old cross where the dearest and best*
*For a world of lost sinners was slain*

They sang together often. Berlon, on his guitar, crooned the melody, and Irene joined in, innately finding the perfect vertical note and the soothing chord.

"That song was mournful, but they sang it so beautifully," said Susan.

*So I'll cherish the old rugged cross*
*Till my trophies at last I lay down*
*And I will cling to the old rugged cross*
*And exchange it some day for a crown.*

I thought back to the note Dad had given me in the 1980s with his handwritten description of Berlon and Irene, the scant family history Wisconsin's adoption services allowed him and Mom to have twenty-five years earlier.

Under the words "Father" Dad had written:

*"Very musically inclined*
*"Can play any instrument"*

Nothing Dad had jotted down about Irene indicated a talent for singing, but the note did say she was artistic and loved to draw.

The little music I heard in our house as a kid came from the television when we watched the Andy Williams Christmas Special or when Mom was inspired to put on a Frank Sinatra or Perry

Como album. But no one ever sang along. I took piano lessons for a while, then picked up the trumpet when I discovered that Dad had played the instrument in high school, but my musical interests were short-lived.

The startling truth was that, for all I was learning about Susan and hearing her stories about growing up on a farm, we still had not met. The drip, drip, drip of her anecdotes about the two people whose blood coursed through my body today promised a river of tales and memories that held the potential to recreate the lives and experiences of two complete strangers. The shrouds that hid these strangers, Irene and Berlon, were now falling away and revealing to me sharper pictures of once-living people whose children—my birth brothers and sisters—I hoped to meet.

Susan had an easy way of telling these stories, with no artifice, no attempt that I could determine to embellish or exaggerate or hide the truth about her mother and father. I wondered if this was innate to who she was. If so, I felt a growing warmth toward her, an easy rapport.

Irene and Berlon were never my parents so I would not know them as a mother and a father. But with every story Susan told me, I sculpted flesh and sinew, I saw gestures and could hear voices where only black-and-white photos and words on a page had been before. I wanted to know more.

## 35

Virtually everything I knew about my birth family I learned from Susan, aside from the details in the adoption report itself. Susan was eager that I should know about everyone, including her younger sister, Jayne.

Jayne, Susan told me in emails and in phone conversations, was deeply religious. A kind of faith that I was only passingly familiar with. Susan's heads-up could have negatively affected my thinking about Jayne, but I tried to remain neutral.

Susan didn't say much to me about Jayne, and I figured out why quickly enough. Susan is openly gay and in a committed relationship of many decades—longer, in fact, than anyone else's marriages among her siblings. My gay pride swelled when I heard that news. I sensed exasperation in Susan's voice when she spoke about Jayne. The tension she felt regarding her sister and probably other family members about their attitude toward her sexuality was deep and long-lived, and as I listened to Susan talk, it was clear to me that the anxiety had become like a millstone she carried around for decades. I could imagine Susan's squelched silences and bit tongues and built-up frustrations when she was among family members who simply did not want to talk about what was right in front of them. Combine this reticence with a deeply ingrained conservative perspective palpable in both family history and geography, and I thought their situation was remarkable for its lack of animosity.

I knew from my own experience what Susan had endured. I came out to my parents when I was nineteen and a freshman at college. And afterward we—Mom, Dad, and I—dropped the subject. What I found both surprising and endearing about my new siblings was that like their relationship with Susan, my family did not talk about my differentness either. But no one stopped talking to me. Susan and I were outliers within our own families, but we were never outcasts.

I thought back to a joke I told my gay friends about Dad. I said that I asked him once which he would have preferred: that I be straight or a Republican. He paused and couldn't answer.

Politics and religion have always been subjects we're told to avoid in polite conversation. In certain circles, you must now add sexuality, which makes a perfect trifecta.

Where Susan was transparent and held back very little in her emails, Jayne was opaque. Susan seemed to be reveling in the news of my existence, whereas Jayne was not fully recovered from the shock.

But she did communicate with me and that was something.

Less than a month after I spoke with both Tony and Chip, I received a call on a Saturday night. It came around 8 p.m. on August 2, 2017. The number that appeared on my phone was not identified, but I answered it anyway. An unfamiliar voice greeted me.

"Hello, this is Jayne. I'm your sister from South Carolina."

It was three hours later in Mullins, a couple miles from Nichols, South Carolina, where she lived. Susan had provided me with photos of Jayne. They shared a family resemblance: an open, round face, high cheekbones, warm, lively eyes, an inviting smile, gleaming teeth. Jayne stood half a head taller than Susan, and her

South Carolina dialect was twangier and more pronounced than Susan's. I was happy to hear from her and I said so.

What I knew about Jayne added up to only a few facts. She was Susan's younger sister, a year older than me. She was a high school guidance counselor.

Had Susan not told me about Jayne's religious beliefs, I knew it would not have mattered. Finding a path to bond with her was my goal. We had only two things in common at this early point on our map: a blood kinship—Irene was my birth mother and Jayne's mother, and we both believed in God. That was more than enough. That's where I started.

"Susan tells me you have a deep faith," I said. "I do, too."

That seemed to open a door. Jayne was happy to tell me about her "walk with God" and I was eager to listen and ask questions. In turn, I was eager to tell her about my faith, my journey.

Jayne told me about her minister. "He started his church in his living room," she said, "with maybe eighteen people. I was one of the first."

"Reverend Michael started Agape the same way," I said.

"We practice the 'casting out' of demons," she said. "It's a moving experience. But people misunderstand what we do."

"I'm not surprised."

Many years earlier, long before I knew about Agape, I had attended a prosperity ministry in Los Angeles led by the singer and actress Della Reese, who was an ordained minister. Her church is called Understanding Principles for Better Living. Reverend Della would talk occasionally about "speaking in tongues," which is a practice indicating one has been filled with the Holy Spirit. One Sunday when Reverend Della was officiating, I witnessed the practice firsthand. Those who were in its hold seemed sincere, but I was skeptical. Although I felt uncomfortable watching them right in front of all of us in the congregation, I accepted that they believed. Looking back on it now, I feel a slight embarrassment at my discomfort. More than anything else, whether you believe or not, speaking in tongues is a literal expression of being in the moment, letting go, being vulnerable. It is a state few human beings allow themselves to experience, including me.

So, when Jayne confessed that her own practices were misunderstood, even though I did not embrace her brand of Christianity myself, I empathized with her. Anyone who stands outside the mainstream experiences this kind of otherness, whether it's one's religion or sexuality.

My story about Reverend Michael Beckwith and Agape may have been as foreign and unnerving to her as hers was to me. But if there was a gap of understanding, I did not let it bother me. I believed after our phone call that Jayne and I connected just enough on that Saturday evening to seal a bond of family. But I could be wrong.

Her emails hinted that she had some work to do in her relationship with Irene. News of my existence came as a shock, and it seemed clear that I may have opened an old wound simply by showing up.

What surprised me was how starkly different my two sisters were and how similar Susan and I were in temperament, outlook, and sexuality. All three of us were connected by blood, even though we were half-siblings.

Who can say why Susan and Jayne took different paths. It's an old debate. The evidence is unambiguous that sexuality is heritable, not a social construct. So that could have been Irene's genetic gift to Susan and me. But the sisters have much else in common. Both chose careers in education. Both are in long-term relationships, although Jayne married, divorced, and is now remarried, while Susan and her partner Judy have been together for more than three decades.

Jayne and I had something else in common: I was working through my feelings about Irene, but I undertook that journey willingly. Jayne, like her siblings, had not volunteered for this adventure. My arrival forced Jayne to reexamine her life and I saw hints of that struggle in her emails. I imagined my other siblings would be traveling a similar path. A path we could navigate together.

## 36

From March 26, the day my sister Jo texted me with news that I could obtain my adoption records, until June 11, when I spoke to Karen Manousos and learned the identity of my birth siblings, I had felt like a passenger on my own journey—in the backseat, along for the ride.

Every day, I said a few words out loud, during my morning prayers, during meditation, even just mumbling to myself as I went about my day: "Let go and let God." These five words are part of what I call my spiritual practices, routine activities I do daily or many times a day to return to or stay in high consciousness. Often, I felt doubtful that I would be able to do this simple thing of letting go. Of turning troubles and events I could not control over to a higher power.

Here, in this life-changing event of first discovering my birth mother and then learning I had birth siblings, I had a slow dawning that the only way I would be capable of navigating the transformations was by doing the very thing I was not sure I could do. But I was in fact letting go. I had to. So much of what had happened, was happening, would be happening, was beyond anything I had experienced.

In *Hamlet*, the "undiscovered country" refers to the afterlife, but I felt as if I were traveling to an undiscovered country without ever leaving my apartment in Los Angeles.

Black is considered by some to be all the colors combined, and if this is true, my emotional state was very dark, but it did not mean I was depressed. I felt like a spelunker dropped into a deep cave, and as much as I hated closed spaces and being in the dark, I had a light. Unexpectedly, the light came from my new birth siblings, not from me. They were taking my phone calls, answering emails, sharing their surprise, even their shock.

But they welcomed me. And they kept the conversation going.

The fear of the unknown I faced as I wavered between whether to read or file the adoption report was real. It's easy to laugh at my quaking now because my indecision lasted only a few days, and in retrospect I found my alarm overblown.

Much more was at stake when I faced this new decision, the decision Jo had chosen against: to connect in a physical setting with my birth siblings.

The fear I felt was tangible, in my gut, in my bones. The cold sweat, the slight but unmistakable nausea I had felt, my trembling fingers as I glanced down at my iPhone before I pressed the button to initiate the call to Karen Manousos, Irene's sister-in-law in Milwaukee. But I pushed the button, and I made the call.

An entirely new fear confronted me in deciding whether to follow Jo's lead or take the step off the ledge into a different kind of unknown. Anyone would be suspicious, adoptee or not, who had the audacity to say they were not afraid of an entire family turning its back on an outsider knocking on their door claiming to be one of them.

My curiosity was piqued by the news that my birth family was bigger than I imagined and about who they were. I was fascinated and grateful that so far, most of them had embraced me. All of them seemed to simply take me at my word, adoption report in hand. If they were waiting for me to announce an agenda—I wanted money, I was homeless and could I move in with one of them—they didn't show it.

What was my sister Jo feeling? She received her adoption records a few weeks before I had. Her birth mother was dead, but she had lived into her eighties before passing only a few years earlier. Like me, Jo had reached out to one or two birth relatives, but she had not yet met any of them. She felt exasperated.

"My friends are more interested in my story than I am," she said one day in a phone call. "I'm tired of telling it."

We laughed about that together.

That frame of mind was not within my sight, and it did not seem on the horizon, but aside from a heightened sense of curiosity about my new siblings, I felt nothing special or remarkable. My therapist opened my eyes.

"Your reactions are not uncommon," she told me. "They will change when you meet your birth family."

I recalled the words of the American Buddhist monk, Pema Chodron, whose books I have read and reread for years.

"The path is uncharted," she wrote in *When Things Fall Apart*. "It comes into existence moment by moment and at the same time drops away behind us."

Susan and I made plans to meet. In September, I had a business trip to Washington, DC. We set a day and time for dinner.

Then Tony emailed to say he wanted to drive from Nichols, South Carolina, north with his wife Marianne to join Susan, her partner Judy and me for the dinner. He signed off, "I want to meet you so much!!"

That Tony would make such a long drive from South Carolina flattered and startled me. Immediately, my emotions changed. A growing anxiety spread throughout my body, and I felt rattled. I wanted to meet Tony and his wife, my new sister-in-law, but now that the prospect was staring me in the face, I told myself I was not ready for it. A quiet evening was defined as

Susan, Judy, and me. But Susan, Judy, Tony, Marianne, and me felt like too much too soon.

Before I arrived at what I thought would be an acceptable and gentle demurring, I wrote multiple drafts of my reply to Tony.

"I am very excited about meeting you and Marianne, too," I wrote in the final draft of my email, "and in fact everyone in my new family, but please understand that my excitement is combined with feeling more than a bit overwhelmed. I set out to find my birth mother and father, and discovered I have an extended family. It's all quite a blessing, but a lot to absorb. That's why I planned to have a quiet visit with Susan and Judy to ease my way into the new situation. Besides, my trip is very short, and your drive would be quite long. There would be little time for getting acquainted. Since you graciously invited me to stay with you in December when I come to Nichols—and that is still my plan—there will be more quiet time for us to get to know one another and share stories and photographs.

"Thank you for being an understanding brother, Tony."

I held my breath and awaited Tony's reply.

"ABSOLUTELY!!" he wrote back, "I understand completely. I agree totally about wanting more time to just sit and talk. Looking forward to December. Marianne is a busy little bee fixing up the house. She has bought a couple old tables and making me refinish them.

"Looking forward!!"

He signed off with "Your brother."

Putting off Tony and Marianne embarrassed me, but I was relieved at how graciously he accepted my request.

I felt a lot of fear and worry. I wanted it to pass, but I also knew it was part of the process.

Some of my gym buddies offered reassurances.

My actor-friend Craig was emphatic. "Don't beat yourself up over this one," he said.

"Your (birth) family is probably as nervous as you are," Rev said. Always the wordsmith, he apparently liked my new birth family's name and greeted me in the morning saying, "What's crackin' McCrackin?"

My sister Linda agreed.

"There's nothing wrong taking this at your own pace," she told me in a phone conversation. "It's a good sign that Tony is so eager to meet you."

## 37

O n the night I met Susan and her partner Judy in the Reston, Virginia, Hilton where I was staying, I sat in my darkened room, dressed in the charcoal gray slacks and V-neck sweater I had worn at my speaking engagement a few hours earlier.

My hotel room was silent. The television was always off when I traveled. I read, constantly. I preferred silence wherever I was, on the road or in Los Angeles. If I turned on the television at home, it was typically on a Sunday to watch something unobtrusive so I could read. PGA golf, volume turned down, was ideal. I bought a separate sound bar to enhance the TV broadcast's audio but if it were left on for more than two hours, it automatically turned itself off. One weekend when I was watching golf, the sound bar went silent, and an hour passed before I noticed.

Silence allowed me to be at peace with my thoughts, undistracted, and that was how I sat in my quiet, unlit hotel room in the moments before I met Susan and Judy. Without warning, shivers gently racked my entire upper body and then were gone as quickly as they had appeared.

"Nerves," I thought. "Definitely nerves."

They were the first and only physical symptoms clueing me

into my emotional state. My body would not let me ignore them, so I stayed seated until a few minutes before we had agreed to meet.

The walk down the long hotel hallway took me to the elevator in an unremarkable space in an unremarkable building, and me in a calmer but unremarkable state. It felt as if I could have been meeting a work colleague for dinner.

As the elevator's glass box descended toward the sitting area, where I told Susan I would meet her, I could see her sitting next to a woman whom I guessed was Judy. Or rather, I could see their forms in the chairs, and the tops of their heads, as the elevator brought me closer to them. They were facing away from me, side by side in those neutrally upholstered chairs that decorate hotel lounges everywhere. The lounge chairs looked the way I felt: beige, blank, a shield I raised when I needed a safety visor.

Without knowing them, I recognized both women. They were in their sixties, only a couple years older than me. As I walked from the elevator, I circled around a row of tall planters that enclosed the sitting area. There she was, sitting. Then she leapt to her feet.

"Hello," I said to my half-sister. Here she was in front of me, the first living relative of a family I had never known, never knew existed. The patriarch and matriarch had died years earlier, the two people I had hoped would be the ones sitting in a pair of chairs somewhere, probably not in a Hilton Hotel outside Washington, DC, but that was a daydream.

Susan looked up at me through wire-framed glasses, her cherub cheeks pressing her happy eyes into slits. A short mop of gray hair, parted on one side, and a big, white-toothed smile, framed her round face. We held each other.

"Hello, brother," she said.

Judy, who was white-haired, slender, and appeared frail and unsteady from a recent health challenge, leaned in for my brief embrace. Her eyes were focused, although her smile, while warm, seemed forced, as if she were posing for a camera. She spoke barely above a whisper. When they stood next to one another, both women were the same height, but Susan projected robustness.

Susan was both familiar and new. The surroundings, forgettable as most hotel decors are, fell away in a blur as I concentrated on the unfamiliar in the familiar: I now have an older sister. Here she was. In front of me. Looking into my eyes. Speaking to me. Shaking my hand. Hugging me.

We took our seats in the dining area and exchanged small talk. I was not nervous, as I expected to be in such an intimate setting. My shivers had fled, and I felt calm, comfortable, at ease.

Susan had something with her, and I did too. I brought along old Ibach family photos to give her some sense of my life. Photos of me less than a month old, as I would have been during my earliest days with Harold and Martha. Photos of my sister Jo, sister Linda, brother Michael, and Mom and Dad. It amounted to a toe dipped into the life of her lost brother, now found.

Susan brought with her a priceless family memento, wrapped in wrinkled, crinkly white tissue paper: a bracelet crafted for a newborn, comprised of a series of off-white beveled square beads on a string with single letters on some of them that spelled out "I am David." In fact, she brought two, so small, so delicate they did not appear real.

"I think these were yours," said Susan in a quiet voice, and I sensed a change in the chemistry of the air around us. The waitstaff and other guests' voices were turned down, the chatter of clinking cutlery and china and goblets hushed for a moment, as if they were privy to a revelation. The room fell away, and Susan and Judy and I were alone, just the three of us.

Susan put one in my left hand. It would have fit on my finger like a ring. I stared at it. I turned to Susan.

"I found them among Momma's things after she died."

Susan had kept them since 1976. She could have told me about them when we spoke on the phone and on video. She had many opportunities to share this familial talisman, but she did not. I understood why she waited. By placing this object in my hand herself, while face-to-face with me, a circle joined ends, a journey completed. The woman whose fingers slipped this bracelet onto my delicate wrist, whose touch I have no memory of, came back to me in the form of the woman, my sister, born to and raised by Irene.

A wave of quiet crested over me and Susan, and revealed to me that my sister and I, both the oldest siblings in our two families, were also rebels in a small way. Both of us declared our differentness, she as a lesbian, I as bisexual. I saw myself in Susan even more than in my blood brothers. Susan and I were linked by DNA, a little less than what I shared with Tony and Chip. But Susan and I were more alike than we were different. Our shared sexuality was not even the obvious bridge, although its revelation startled and made complete sense. My half-sister and I were two people separated by geography, six decades, vast cultural differences, yet our bond was undeniable.

Nothing would ever separate Susan and me.

My forefinger traced the edge of this tiny item, and I did not know what to say. I swallowed, shaking my head in disbelief.

Within my thirty-three-page adoption report was a photocopy of a birth certificate with the name David Small typed on it. So many documents had been assembled and shipped off to me whose purpose was to prove that I had been born to Irene Manousos McCrackin more than sixty years earlier.

But this. This piece of baby jewelry. This aged yet almost new declaration. I never had any doubts, not one, that Irene was the woman who bore me, that this family was my birth family, and that Susan, sitting next to me in a Hilton Hotel dining room in Reston, Virginia, was my sister. A blood relative.

Yet this token with the words "I am David" beneath my finger reduced all my paper evidence to virtual irrelevance. Nothing more than the almost weightless oval bracelet I now lifted and put back in my left palm mattered, these petite beads on a soft cotton string.

How did Irene acquire them? Even if, as I suspect, she found them in the hospital gift shop in Milwaukee, it spoke to me of her mindfulness, her intentions. She must have known her time with me would be short, a few breaths, a few blinks of an eye, a few smiles, stifled tears, and I would be gone.

All these thoughts rushed through my brain.

"I wanted you to have them," said Susan, but I hardly heard her speak.

The bracelet was a marvel, a piece of my history, and I placed it on the dining table next to my cell phone.

I recalled how my therapist had told me not to worry that I felt nothing. That this would change. She was right. Here was a tiny and tangible confirmation that connected me to Irene. She had slipped both of these breathtakingly small items onto my minutes-old wrists where they remained probably for less time than I had been alive before she had to remove them and...my imagination was carrying me away...she literally lifted me from her lap where she was lying in her hospital bed and placed me in the arms of someone—a nurse, a social worker—who turned and walked out of her room. With me in her arms.

Irene never saw me again.

That scene flashed in my head and a tinge of metal filled my mouth as adrenaline coursed briefly through my body. I was not sad or hurt or angry. I touched the bracelet and wondered what Irene might have felt in that moment of letting go. My imagination failed me.

And I never saw the bracelet again.

Susan and Judy and I talked and swapped stories for an hour and a half. We took selfies and group photos with the help of the wait staff and sent copies off to my youngest birth brother, Chip, whose birthday fell on that day.

At the end of the evening, I gathered up my phone and the envelope of photos I had brought and walked Susan and Judy to their car. Susan and I planned to spend most of the next day wandering around the National Mall in Washington, DC., continuing the process of getting to know one another.

My phone buzzed with a new text at 7:43 pm. It was from Susan.

"Did you pick up the baby bracelet? Judy thought she saw it on the table."

My reaction was instant: hand to forehead forcefully, I threw on my shoes and raced to the hotel dining room. It was open, but empty and quiet. Our table had already been cleared, cleaned, and reset with new linen and flatware. I searched the floor, all around, but saw nothing.

Next, I flagged a waiter and asked who had cleared our table. The poor soul appeared in a few seconds, and I spelled out the crisis. He was panic-stricken, clearly understanding what I had lost and directed me to the kitchen area. There he donned surgical gloves and pointed to three almost-human-sized trash bins.

Bless his heart, he spent the next forty minutes bent over, first one, then another, emptying all three down to their slimy bottoms.

He would not stop apologizing and I could not stop saying thank you for his thankless efforts. I rewarded him with a generous tip.

But the bracelet was gone.

I called Susan when I got back to my room. She deserved that rather than a text. She was clearly devastated, but philosophical.

The next morning, I awoke to find another text from her, written at 3:16 a.m.

"There isn't a chance you picked it up with the pictures, is there? Regardless, you can have the other one."

I poured over the small packet of photographs to see if I had picked up the bracelet unknowingly. Nothing.

"No, you keep the other bracelet," I said to her later that morning as we began our day exploring the National Mall in Washington, DC. "I saw it and held it in my hands. I also have the photos you sent me." I was content. The memory of the delicate object was enough.

There would be no omen-like significance attached to this disappointment.

"I won't allow it to spoil our first meeting," I said to Susan as we set out.

"Me neither," she said, looking me in the eye so I could tell she meant what she said. "A door closes, a window opens."

That is how I saw it too. And I felt a kinship with a kindred spirit. My birth sister and I shared an optimism about the world.

## 38

Two days after I returned to Los Angeles from my visit with Susan in Reston, Virginia, in September 2017, I started making plans to visit the McCrackins in Nichols, South Carolina over Christmas.

Life is about timing, being available and in the moment. Reverend Michael told me that I chose to be born. I struggled to understand this idea, but I did not dismiss it. If this notion were true, that I chose to arrive on the planet where and when I did, some might argue that my timing was less than perfect. In Irene's life, I showed up between husbands: after Junior died, and before she agreed to marry her second husband, my birth father, Berlon.

But that was not my perspective. My timing was perfect. I grew up with Martha and Harold, which is where I wanted to be all along.

"You're with who you chose to be with," Reverend Michael said to me. I believed he believed what he said even if I had difficulty grasping the idea. But I still hear his words as if he spoke them yesterday.

Now, in the reverie of embracing one birth sibling for the first time, I made plans to meet Jayne, Tony, John, Chip and the many aunts, uncles, cousins, and other relatives who called Nichols,

South Carolina and vicinity, their home. I felt a rising anticipation to hear more stories about Berlon and Irene.

My path was already disappearing behind me, well-traveled and in the past, as Pema Chodron explained. What came next, I could not see, but I knew it would be there. All I had to do was take another step.

## 39

Tony McCrackin and his wife Marianne lived about five miles outside Nichols, South Carolina. Tony also owned a cabinet-making business, and his studio/workshop was on family land across the narrow highway from his home. For some reason my GPS app, Waze, decided the studio was his house. I knew it was a mistake. I'd zoomed in on Google Earth Pro and saw his house a week before I boarded my plane in Los Angeles. I saw his studio, too, across the road. I saw it, right in front of my eyes.

The address I plugged into Waze for Tony and Marianne McCrackin's house was correct and as I approached the building in my rental, I saw only a few hundred feet down the road was, in fact, a correct address. Just not *the* correct address.

And still I made the wrong turn when I knew I was going in the wrong direction.

Why did I do that? My last-minute unconscious warning system blaring in my head? If so, it was a lame buzzer because I was committed. No turning back.

I turned around in Tony's studio's drive and headed back to the highway and the house, on the left, where I knew I should have headed in the first place. Susan and Tony emerged from the front door as I pulled into the driveway and waited for me on the deck.

My heart was pounding, but the sight of Susan's familiar smile was a relief. I hugged her as soon as I stepped out of my car. Tony came up next and gave me a bearhug.

Not home, exactly. But it was the beginning, which was home by another name. Susan and Tony's greeting turned out to be the tenor of my visit. They welcomed me as if I had only been away for a long trip. As if nothing were a surprise. As if I had always belonged.

But the weight of what I was about to do had not yet hit me: plunging head-first into a new and unfamiliar tribe in a part of the world that was foreign to me. My meeting with Susan three months earlier was easy because we had connected in many ways many times before the dinner. The dinner itself was on neutral territory, my hotel restaurant.

Now, however, I had traveled to territory, ground zero, so to speak, of all things McCrackin, their family home, where Irene and Berlon were buried. I wanted to drive by the Jones Dairy to witness for myself the spot where Junior had been killed in 1955, where the wheels of my life had been set in motion.

Talking on the phone with Tony and Chip, and later with Jayne, kept everything in a kind of abstraction, a single dimension. Their voices were real, but I had to imagine everything else. I had seen their photos, so there was a picture of them in my mind. But I had Skyped only with Susan and met her for dinner and the day after wandered around the National Mall in DC the way friends, or siblings, do when they get together.

My emotional confusion did not surprise me. It wasn't butterflies in my stomach so much as a rumbling in my gut. Butterflies would have been welcomed. I wasn't afraid, I told myself. I wasn't trespassing. They invited me, after all.

Then I paused and let the truth seep in. I *was* afraid. I *was* scared. But I was also prepared to allow myself to feel all of it, to lean into it and not let my fears stop me.

More later than in the moment, I recognized that I wanted to finish this personal journey, to culminate a decision I had made barely nine months earlier, yet I felt the fight-or-flight switch flip on, and I hurtled down an interior road riddled with S-curves that I'd traveled many times.

I felt out of control, but I didn't know what control felt like.

My sister Jo had driven twenty minutes from her home in Phoenix to visit the younger brother of her late birth mother. Her birth uncle and his wife. The physical distance required hardly more effort than going to the grocery store, but I have no doubts she felt as if she were crossing the Grand Canyon on a tight rope.

My ninety-one-year-old father, Harold, never uttered a word of objection to either Jo or me when we told him about our plans to write to Wisconsin for our adoption records and then to track down living birth relatives. He was eager to hear the latest news every time one of us called him in Austin.

Everyone in my circle—my siblings, my friends, acquaintances, and work colleagues—loved hearing about the adventure I was on.

Yet I could not hide the little tremors of fear welling up in me. My circle sensed these fears too.

"Rent a car so you can leave if things get weird," an LA friend texted me a few weeks before I departed.

On a long phone call with an old friend in Chicago, I heard this advice: "Stay only a couple days."

"Get a hotel room," said a gay couple, in unison, whom I'd known since we met in Milwaukee more than thirty years earlier.

Linda, in full lawyer mode, warned: "Avoid talking politics at all costs."

For the first time since I began attending Agape International Spiritual Center, I put in a prayer request for the Sunday before I left. In fact, I handed the request directly to Reverend Michael at the gym on Friday. I asked simply for his and the community's blessings for a safe trip.

My wrong turn toward Tony's cabinet-making studio may

have revealed some unconscious fears, but I made it to his house. Into Susan's embrace. Into Tony's welcoming hug.

As soon as I stepped inside Tony and Marianne's home, which had been Berlon and Irene's home before them, the aroma of Marianne's spicy, fragrant Christmas kitchen triggered memories of Bayside when I was growing up. Marianne would arrive from work an hour or so later. In the meantime, Tony launched immediately into showing me around the place and we walked the grounds of the family homestead, a small remnant of the original farm Berlon had taken over years earlier. Susan, Tony, and I were standing at the edge of the property a few hundred yards from the house, looking deep into the thick woods at the crumbling remains of some outbuilding, with Tony playing docent, when I heard footsteps crunching the ground behind me. I turned and saw Chip.

"Hello brother," he said, a huge grin on his open face. Without missing a step, his arms swallowed me.

When Marianne arrived, I received yet another warm embrace. But then she startled me.

"I bet you expected to see an old pickup up out front on cement blocks," she said after releasing me. She was smiling, but her eyes were blank. I could not read her expression.

I smothered my ironic ad-guy retort.

"No," I said, trying my best to be jovial, looking at Tony, then Susan, then Chip, but not at Marianne. "Not really."

Marianne and Tony had almost married years earlier but found each other again after their first marriages failed. It's a toss-up over who, between husband and wife, had the strongest South Carolina dialect. Marianne's was more melodic. She also shared Tony's mischievous eyes, which, once she felt comfortable with me, lit up when she smiled.


"So, let's take a drive around Nichols," Tony announced.

The five of us, me, Marianne, Chip, and Tony, climbed into

Tony's SUV and started a tour of the geography, the farms, the neighborhood. Susan disappeared to visit a favorite aunt who lived nearby. The word "neighborhood" didn't quite define the area. My boyhood home in Bayside was located in a classic neighborhood. Same with my home in Silver Lake, a hilly and leafy community carved out of Los Angeles. We were in Horry County, pronounced ore-EE, and just speaking it aloud makes you feel Southern. Nichols spreads out endlessly, or so it seemed to an urban dweller like me. I had to call it what it was: rural. Something else I had to get used to.

"Someone please point out the Jones Dairy," I said, speaking to no one, once we were out driving around, "if we go past it."

The Jones Dairy was sacred ground for me. The circumstances that led to Irene and Berlon getting pregnant with me began on the cold, hard pavement of Nichols Highway in the presence of the Jones Dairy. Irene and Berlon were both gone. But the event that brought them together, George Watson's eighteen-wheel logging truck that slammed into Junior's passenger car, an explosion of shrieking tires, metal and glass twisting and shattering unnaturally, propelled Irene and Berlon in a direction they most likely did not expect.

I had to see this place.

"We just went by it," said Chip, who was sitting behind me.

"What?!" I said, turning around in my seat and looking back, but I would not have seen it even if I saw it. Because I had never seen it. We had rounded a slight curve in the road.

"We'll come back," said Tony, behind the wheel. "Don't you worry."

We had driven past the farm, the buildings, a landscape ripe with meaning and symbolism. All of that was in the rear-view mirror before I realized what had transpired. The path fell away behind me. I turned to face forward.

My siblings knew this ground. They'd been over it countless times. Unlike me, the McCrackins were on another drive on another day.

. . .

TONY TAUGHT me the difference between a graveyard and a cemetery. A graveyard is connected to a church, while a cemetery is not and is typically smaller. We stopped at many cemeteries, but not a single graveyard.

My birth family began the slow process of introducing me to my old family, relatives long since perished, laid to rest in cemeteries all around Nichols and nearby Mullins. Some of these resting grounds were tiny, taking up no more space than a couple basketball courts. Tony knew where they were, but as we drove, I lost my bearings. A turn, another turn, then another cemetery.

We parked on a shoulder at the edge of another lonely country road and began a walk among and between tall headstones. I saw the McCrackin family name appear, first here and there, then taking up rows. I noticed some spelling variations and Chip made what I gathered was an oft-told joke about who was whom based on which spelling. I laughed too. Those whose names ended in "in," like us, were the smart ones, he said. Those that ended in "en" were good-looking. Or was it the other way around?

Small, faded Confederate flags were everywhere, on thin, reedy wood sticks pushed into the ground next to so many names, including McCrackin family headstones. Both spellings. I wanted to say something because I objected to the flag. This flag. Its presence offended me, but I bit my tongue. I was a guest. Mom and Dad had taught me manners, and I knew better.

As quickly as I let go of this dark feeling, something else came over me, something deeper.

"I envy what you have in this small, close-knit community, with family—living and dead—so close," I said. "A sense of place. Deep roots."

My unfinished thought caught in my throat, and I choked up. The tears came upon me, and I could not stop them. Chip put his arm around my shoulder, then Tony and Marianne joined us. I felt hands on my back, on my arm. I breathed deeply and said nothing more.

Here, all around me, were the remains of a family dating back well before the Civil War. My Ibach family's loved ones, in contrast, were spread out over many states and many cemeteries. I am not friends with envy, but I felt its tug this day. In only minutes, Tony had navigated his vehicle over a few miles of country roads and in that time, I saw evidence of almost two centuries of McCrackin family roots. What a stark contrast to my family in Wisconsin. It hit me hard.

We were quiet, standing on a gravel shoulder looking out at row after row of markers of family gone, but never far away. Strangers, but blood kin. Touching each other in flesh and in spirit. The other side of the thin veil now gently pierced.

## 40

"Do you want to see where Momma and Daddy are buried?" said Tony.

"Yes," I said, "of course."

This was the final stop on our drive past the farms and the cemeteries and on the country roads around Nichols on my first day with my new siblings, Tony, his wife Marianne, and Chip. Susan would join us later back at the McCrackin family home.

Our destination was Cedar Creek Cemetery, a lonely, barren plot of land on the crest of a hill, surrounded by scrawny brush and farmland bordering three sides. It was December. Brown and beige compacted earth, dry and dusty, colored the wan canvas of this quiet and forlorn site. Some grass had been planted around the burial stones, but it struggled and, in many spots, had failed to make a home in the earth. Irene and Berlon were buried here.

Each heavy granite stone sat a few inches above patchy dirt mixed with pale green dying grass at a slight angle, like a lectern. The neat rows suggested a well-planned layout, but the contrasting faded grass recalled the forgotten.

The markers, both rectangular, were made of granite, cut with a rough edge, and made to appear like a framed picture. The outer two inches, like matting, was a pale rose. Two deeply etched dark lines, one inside the other, framed the paler off-white granite within. Here is where I saw the names of my birth parents. The markers sat side by side. The marker on the right read "Irene M. McCrackin," and above it was her nickname in quotation marks: Butch. Two feet to the left the marker read "Berlon McCrackin." Looking up, I scanned the distant sloping landscape.

The brisk weather chilled me, and I felt strangely satisfied. Here was the "movie" ending, the resting place of my birth mother and birth father, where an actor playing the part of the adoptee stands and his tears fall to the parched earth...

Cut.

For half a sec, this scene played in my head, but I swiped it away quickly. It was not disrespectful. It was inaccurate. My emotions wavered because the moment felt so casual, informal. My birth siblings had been here many times and I assumed they had processed their grief long ago. They were mingling together, not looking at the markers or anything, as if they were bored and waiting for me.

This was my first visit, a trip of many firsts, and this was the latest first. For me this piece of land was not sacred, but still special. I was not connected to the dirt but to the people buried beneath it.

That image, "buried beneath," summarized much of what I was feeling or trying to understand about my feelings. For so many months leading up to my visit to this out-of-the-way corner of South Carolina, I was trying to dig deeper, peel away the years of incuriosity about this part of my history. For those adoptees who felt incomplete, a moment like this may have brought solace. I did not feel that emptiness and I was not here to grieve. I was here to discover, to learn and add to a long and wondrous narrative I began the day after Irene handed me over to a social worker in Mt. Sinai Hospital in Milwaukee, twenty-six days after Harold and Martha welcomed me into the Ibach family.

These moments brought satisfaction. More than that, I felt awe. What was next? What would my satisfaction bring to me?

Absence from this place and these moments were necessary before I could grasp the meaning and significance of the wonder that emerged in my heart on this cold afternoon. As the historian Robert Caro has said, "Time equals truth." Time would let the experiences of this day and this weekend trip to Nichols sink in and reveal their mysteries.

Was I at the end of my journey as I stood in a barren cemetery on a Friday afternoon under a brilliant blue sky? Nine months earlier, I had sent off an old-fashioned bank check and a completed two-page application to the state of Wisconsin. A few weeks later, I had a thirty-three-page adoption report with a name and a story.

The search for my birth mother came down to the most unlikely spot on earth where the woman who bore me, and the man who fathered me, now lay.

Who could have possibly prepared me for this?

And then I remembered Pema Chodron's words. My travel to this place was never intended to be my "destination," a period at the end of a sentence. It was always going to be a comma.

## 41

Later that night, before we went out for a family dinner, I sat on the edge of the bed in Tony and Marianne's guest bedroom, and I wondered why I had cried at the cemetery overflowing with McCrackin headstones—both spellings. As I've grown older, my emotions have moved closer to the surface. I have never been afraid to cry, but these tears came over me with no warning.

My feelings were not provoked by the one cemetery, but by all of them we had visited that day. The accumulation of these small resting places filled with McCrackins induced a momentary loss of my composure. It seemed out of left field, but I could not dispute my feelings. Here, in a few hundred square yards of rich, South Carolina farmland, a congregation of loved ones were gathered and laid out neatly, an everyday reminder of ancient blood surrounded by ancestral lands. Family history marked by a host of stones.

That was foreign to me, so many similar names going back more than a century, back to the 1840s, all in one place. So what if some names ended in "en" and others in "in." It wasn't the spellings that startled me. The family name appeared everywhere I turned. *Everywhere.* I had never witnessed anything like it before.

As I sat on the bed in the home of my birth family, a structure that had been the center of the world for McCrackins for more than eighty years, recalling the maze of cemeteries I had walked over, I could not help feeling groundless. All the names I saw that day served to construct for my birth family a history I did not share. It was mine by a real, but tenuous connection to a family who resided here for centuries. But it was not my history. It never would be.

And what *was* my history?

The Ibach family, at least my little sliver of it, began with my great-grandfather, Peter Ibach, who arrived in St. Louis, Missouri, from Germany in 1878 at the age of sixteen. He migrated north to Alma, Wisconsin, a village on the Mississippi where he married my great-grandmother, Matilda Laue, in 1887. They had three children, my great uncle Sydney, my grandfather, Herbert, and my great-aunt, Esther. Sydney never married and died in this fifties. Esther lived into her nineties, and never married. Only my grand-father Herbert married and had children, my dad and his brother, Paul. Dad and Mom, and my Uncle Paul and his wife each raised four children, but the Ibach tribe that planted roots in America with Peter 145 years ago ends with me, my siblings, and my cousins because my brother died at eighteen, and I and my two male cousins did not produce a male child to carry on the next generation.

Nothing could be starker than to realize that my family has a beginning, a middle and an end, like a home movie spinning on its take-up reel.

I grabbed for something, anything. I felt myself drifting. Tony, Chip, and Susan planted their own roots decades earlier in this very soil. So had all their siblings and family members and long-dead ancestors. Nichols, South Carolina, was not merely home. It was sacred ground.

Did I have such a place in my life? Not the same way that my birth siblings experienced it in Nichols. But two days later, on my flight back to Los Angeles, images from Jonathan Lane and the ravine around my boyhood home came back to remind me that I was not adrift. Was all of that truly sacred ground? Yes, but my sacred ground was not long-held family land, nor a cemetery where relatives were buried.

My sacred ground was the remembered crackling snow underfoot as Jo, Mike, Linda, and I trod out our front door and walked to the bus stop to go to school in December. The ascending growl of the lawn mower starting up on Saturday mornings in June. Mom's cocoa-bean mulch scenting the air in April.

Memories. More than I could count.

## 42

On all my visits to Nichols, and I made four between 2017 and 2019, I was an over-night guest in the house Berlon and Irene lived in and on the land they cultivated, which now belonged to Tony and Marianne. I always slept in Tony and Marianne's guest room, what had once been Berlon and Irene's bedroom. They had not slept in the same bed since August 1976, when Irene died. Berlon passed away twenty-seven years later.

The experience of sleeping in the bedroom my birth parents shared was like stepping into a time machine and not having to go anywhere. As soon as I walked into the room, I was confronted by two items hanging on the wall above the bed: an old Alex banjo, which was a gift from Berlon and Irene to Tony when he was thirteen, and a 1942 C.F. Martin guitar, which Berlon acquired in 1945, when he would have been nineteen. In between the two instruments, Marianne hung a framed print of a painting depicting a guitar in the foreground, surrounded by white hydrangeas and in the background, a revival tent meeting with a music sheet and the first four bars of "Precious Memories" superimposed in the center of the image.

These instruments were now relics, displayed on the wall

above the bed where my birth father had slept. Tony demonstrated the family musicality when he brought down the banjo to play for a few minutes on that visit. Years earlier, when Berlon was alive, Tony said that he had joined his daddy from time to time on a Saturday night to play with other friends at a local honky tonk.

The bed was suitable for one person, intimate for a couple.

"You slept in your parents' bed?" my gym buddy Craig, the actor, asked after I'd returned from the 2017 Christmas trip.

"No," I corrected, smiling, "not my parents, my birth parents."

"Okay, sorry," he said, a little miffed, "your *birth* parents. But you slept in their bed? Wasn't that, you know, creepy?"

It was not creepy I reassured my inquisitive friend. In fact, I was surprised at how not creepy it felt. Standing at the foot of the bed I did a slow pan around the room like a movie camera, etching the imagery into my memory.

"Could you see yourself living there?" Craig asked. Like so many of my friends, Craig was always eager to hear news about my journey and he was one of the few whose interest and questions never bothered me. My sister Jo had said she grew weary of these kinds of questions from her friends, and I understood, but Craig knew intuitively when to ask and when to move on.

"You know," I said, eyeing him carefully, pausing to see if he was serious or kidding and decided he was serious. "That feeling never came over me. I felt like a visitor. Welcome, but just a visitor."

"Oh, c'mon," he pushed, and I let him. "You had to feel something."

Yeah, I had felt something. One of the reasons I liked Craig so much was that he was an actor and actors love to wrestle with their emotions. Emotions are their stock in trade. Even when he was hired for a television commercial, he tried to tap into his character's in-the-moment feelings.

"I was surprised when Tony showed me into the bedroom and

told me whose it was," I said. "I was stunned to be standing there. All these family photos, everywhere around me."

I hadn't anticipated being ushered into this room. Where I would be staying was not that important, only that I would be Tony and Marianne's guest. These details, whose bedroom was whose, were far too granular for me when I had been invited to visit. I went where I was led, and I was trying to be an accommodating guest.

And then, there I was. Irene and Berlon had slept here. In the bed I reached out and touched. And then I slept in it myself.

"Same mattress?" asked Craig. Now he was smiling down at me from his six-foot-something height, his eyes crinkled, his baritone clearly jesting with me.

"Now you're creeping *me* out," I shot back, and we shared a laugh.

"Did you feel their eyes on you?" he asked.

"You mean my siblings?"

"Yeah," he said. "Were they watching you for a reaction?"

"I never thought about that," I said, a little surprised by the question. "But no, I couldn't tell."

Tony and Marianne may have been watching me. I was the stranger in their house. I posed no threat, but how the hell would they know that? They had drawn their own conclusions about me the same way I had drawn conclusions about them. We read each other, first over the phone, then face-to-face and arrived at a similar spot: we each saw the other as new, a little different, but comfortable and on-the-tip-of-your-tongue vaguely familiar.

# 43

How do you get to know a brother who is fifty-six years old when you meet him for the first time? He was a stranger. If Irene had not given me up for adoption and I had been raised with all the McCrackins, Tony would have arrived in the household when I was four. He would have been a stranger even then. Okay, not quite the same scenario. He would have been a blank slate not a stranger. I would have learned about him, and he about me, in that slow process called "growing up together."

But that's not the way it happened. Not for me and Tony or any of my siblings, half or full. Tony was in fact my "full brother," one whom I shared the same birth mother and birth father with. And there the similarities ended. He was my brother, but he lived in a place and in circumstances as different from mine as I could imagine.

Yes, Tony McCrackin is my full brother, but who says "full brother" these days? It was awkward, ungainly, and ultimately unnecessary. He is *my brother,* and I grew accustomed to saying it to him and he said it to me. He said it without a second thought, and I responded.

"Hello, brother" was his usual greeting in a text or on the

phone. I credit Tony for kick-starting this ritual, the beginning of a bonding between two people separated by decades, geography and experience. The first pile driven deep into the bedrock that eventually became a solid bridge that connected us. Me and Tony. But not just me and Tony. Me and Tony and Chip. But not John, the middle McCrackin brother. John decided not to connect with me, so I have never met him, heard his voice, or received a text or email from him. Only he knows his reasons. My new siblings told me that John has cut himself off from the family. They have offered me some explanations, but I will not share them here. John deserves the right to tell me his story firsthand, and someday I believe he will.

There's something that makes bonding between brothers different from bonding between sisters and I don't think it matters whether it's half or full sisters. Susan was also three years older than me and that had something to do with it, too. I'd never had an older sister, especially an older sister who was gay. I did not come out to her as quickly as she did to me, and I know that speaks to my own fears. She told me she and Judy both knew about me even before I confided in her. We always seem to know even before words are spoken.

Brothers are a different department. If bonding with a sister is like reading poetry, where she and I navigate by feel and impressions and perceptions, bonding with brothers is akin to reading an essay: This is who I am, and this is what I think. Each brother presents a premise supported with facts. It's not nearly as dry and humorless as it sounds, not when your brother is Tony at any rate. If Tony were an essay, he'd have been written by Dave Barry.

Tony is what's called a "master" cabinet maker. He is a highly skilled woodworker. Whether he uses hand tools hundreds of years old or the latest in computer-aided design, Tony can build cabinets and furniture from any blueprint or none at all. I always found it odd that someone of Tony's mastery would be called "good with his hands." That was true, of course, but his hands were merely the instruments of his talent. They were inspired by his heart, his creativity, and his well-ordered brain. Tony would say he was inspired by God and his hands were following orders, and I would agree.

Tony's cabinet and woodworking studio sat on McCrackin farmland across the street from the family home, next to a man-made pond, roughly a half-acre, shaped like a giant strip of bacon, a little crooked in the middle. That's how it appeared on Google Maps from overhead. A towering South Carolina pine lords over the pond on its eastern shore.

On my first visit to Nichols in 2017, Tony and I walked around the pond and I stood next to this tree, which soared fifty feet and cast a long shadow on a clear, chilly Saturday morning in December. I marveled at it, its base and trunk twisted, as if it had been in a fight to lay claim to this spot of land and wore its scars with pride.

Tony texted his brother, sisters, and me a meditation about the old tree, revealing a talent with words I had not known about.

"I see this old pine tree every day of my life," he texted. "I'm third generation on this farm.

"My dad almost lost this farm after a record drought in 1954. Nineteen fifty-five brought hope with the digging of this irrigation pond. According to my dad, the pine survived the dragline that dug the pond because it was such a small sprout. Daddy let it grow."

I walked the circumference of the South Carolina pine at the edge of the pond with Tony, and put my hands on its cold, rough, wrinkled bark. Its mangled appearance belied how solid and sturdy it felt, how it held its ground despite its earlier near-death wrestling match with Berlon's dragline.

"It's the victim of a trauma," Tony wrote, "that a dragline puts a small tree through."

Tony taught Sunday school at his church, and I began to hear the teacher in him and the true nature of my brother's heart as well. I could almost see him standing in front of a small group of youngsters, whose attention would be easily riveted by this man.

When Tony told a story, his entire body became part of the tale. He'd bob his head, lean in, and pause at the right moment, his eyes bulging, eyebrows raised. He would remain silent for effect and then like a well-timed exhale, he'd deliver the moral.

"Life is very much like this old pine," he wrote in this text. "We cannot control where we're planted. We're often traumatized, and we weather storms. None of these things are avoidable.

"The only thing we can control is how we react to these inconveniences."

Inconveniences. I liked his choice of words.

Tony and I may have been born five years apart and lived thousands of miles from each other, raised in entirely different places, entirely different families, but we shared what all humans share. The loss of a loved one, estrangements from family, disappointments, setbacks. Tony and I both had our fair share. But he chose to describe such inevitable heartaches as...inconveniences.

So, we shared a common attitude of resilience and perseverance. And a requisite sense of humor.

And then Tony added lines from Jeremiah 17, verses 7 and 8:

> "Blessed is the man that trusted in the Lord
> And wise hope the Lord is.
> For he shall be as a tree
> Planted by the waters,
> And that spreadeth out her roots by the river.
> And shall not see when heat cometh,
> But her leaf shall be green;
> And shall not be careful in the year of drought,
> Neither shall cease from yielding fruit."

Tony concluded: "Like this old pine on my farm, we need to be planted by the water. The Living Water of Hope."

. . .

IRENE AND BERLON waited for four years after me to have more children. Why did they wait so long? It is not hard to believe they were deeply in love. In a new marriage, four years seems like an eternity. How did they manage?

Irene did not get pregnant again until spring 1960 and gave birth to Tony in January 1961. It is not unreasonable to conclude that some...insurmountable obstacle emerged between them in the early years of their marriage, resulting in a four-year delay in having more children. They must have talked about it—sex, children. Or it's possible they avoided the subject. No one can know. But it piques one's curiosity.

At that time, Berlon's first and only son—me—had been born and given away while he was in South Carolina and Irene was back home in Wisconsin. It's impossible to know how much Berlon knew about Irene's plans to put me up for adoption. He may have known in advance. Did he approve? He barely allowed himself to acknowledge my existence when Susan pressed him about me many years later, and then erected a permanent wall of silence on the topic, a conversation that took place after Irene's death, when Susan was in college. My guess is that Berlon did not approve of Irene's decision.

And I became the family secret.

Tony welcomed me as if he had known me for years.

That, I was to learn quickly, was Tony. He was gregarious, rarely without a smile, and when he was not smiling his eyes were. His face was a Broadway marquee of his emotions, but I knew his mask was as intricately constructed as any piece of wood he had shaped into a claw-footed dining table.

Tony loved to plead ignorance about what was on his docket on a given weekend day.

"Marianne will tell me what I need to do," he'd say. "I just go where she points."

This Saturday, I played the role of Tony's assistant on an errand to deliver an ornate mahogany buffet to a client for whom he had done much work. It was oversized and bulky and as solid wood, it was also heavy. My arrival was propitious. Tony needed me to help him lift the buffet onto a wheeled pallet he had built for the purpose of moving such objects like this one and then move it onto his custom-made trailer.

I thought I'd seen just about every kind of towed vehicle known to humanity, but I have never seen anything remotely resembling Tony's woodworking studio-on-wheels. On the outside, you'd be forgiven for mistaking it for a horse trailer, minus windows. Measuring at least twenty-feet long, eight-feet wide and almost seven-feet tall on the inside, this trailer was a moveable feast of the tools of his trade. It was a pared down version of his studio.

When we returned from his delivery errand, Tony introduced me to the real thing. The imposing prefab rectangular building measured roughly forty by sixty feet, with a twenty-foot peaked ceiling. The container itself was off-the-shelf. Its contents, the scent of sawdust, oiled blades, paints and stains and ideas for cabinets, chairs, tables, and other pieces of furniture were custom-designed to suit its owner's demanding specs. Even items he did not build but existed as sketches on random pieces of notepaper were held in place on a wall by a monster clip. Nothing was discarded. As a writer, I did the same thing with drafts of my writing. File them away, but don't throw them away.

Walking around his studio was like touring Tony's brain. I could see how he thought by the way the space was laid out. The system he had developed—drawers lined up a certain way, low-slung cabinets on wheels slipped neatly under a worktable, finishing tools here, old blades there—was his own, but I could see he had a system.

He played guide for me. He walked me around his tidy work-space while he recited what his youthful, and sometimes not so youthful, errors had taught him about designing, executing, and building the hundreds, perhaps thousands, of wood projects commissioned by friends, neighbors, strangers-soon-to-be-friends, and other referrals over the years. What Tony learned about his craft taught me about the man. He was not educated the way I had been by going to college and graduate school, but he and I shared what anyone who values education wants most: he had learned how to learn. As I listened to his anecdotes about the space he had created where he did his work, he revealed matter-of-factly the insights and lessons, occasionally painfully wrought, that accumulated like wrinkles.

Tony's recollections were a museum of his "mistakes corrected."

At any of the dozen or so workstations laid out in rows, Tony would point to a die-cut stacked like a book nested in a slot on a wall that he designed to hold old die cuts. Or he pulled open a drawer and showed me a tool.

"I used this, oh, twenty years ago. A fella wanted six dining chairs," he said, turning the tool over in his hands. "I'd tried it but couldn't get it to do what I wanted."

"Why do you still have it?" I asked.

"I might find a use for it," he said.

Whether it's a tool Tony stored away or a few paragraphs I'd cut from an essay and saved in a file on my desktop, some things we did not discard.

Tony shared a couple more stories like that. In drawers, on shelves, hanging from the walls, just about everywhere in his studio were examples of ideas that worked and some that didn't, all stored away for reference.

"I don't like to repeat mistakes," he said, a smile on his face meant not so much for me as for himself.

The walls of his studio were prefabricated, but just about everything within those walls was designed by Tony or refashioned in some way to suit his requirements. Some of these details, which I would have walked past without noticing, he would stop and point to. The nooks for his old die cuts were only one example.

"You see that workbench?" he said, resting his right hand on a table. "I fastened caster wheels on it so I could move the whole thing around rather than have to carry a half dozen items back and forth to the table saw."

These were ingenious ideas to me, the novice, the uninitiated. To Tony, they were problems solved. He was always thinking four, five, six steps ahead.

"You'll never catch me playing chess with you anytime soon," I said.

"I've never played chess before," he replied, unable to hide his Cheshire grin.

Yeah. And I was not going to be the one to teach him.

## 44

Chip was the youngest McCrackin sibling, born to Irene and Berlon in September 1964. When he claimed he had no memory of his mother, Irene, I never believed him. He was not a liar nor was he deluding himself. He believed he was telling the truth. Between our many phone calls and later when the family and I got together and reminisced about the old days, as we did on my first visit to Nichols, Chip's faulty memory revived. Sooner or later, he'd make his way to a recollection about Irene. Stories emerged. Many about his life as a boy on the family farm. Some about his mother.

He was his mother's son and easily the most profoundly hurt by her premature death.

"I was in therapy for a long time," he admitted to me in our first phone conversation. That was a scary thing to say, especially to a stranger, even if I was his new brother. So I felt an easy warmth begin to form around us.

"How are you now?" I asked.

"Oh, I'm fine."

How many times have I heard that? How many times have I spoken those very words myself, and not meant a syllable of it? I wondered if Chip meant it. He had good reason not to.

The anguish in his voice, and on his face, softened him in my eyes. His vulnerability made it impossible for me not to like him. Chip was not tall, no taller than I was, but he was muscular and bearish with a calm demeanor. He spoke in clipped phrases, never rushed. He did not show his teeth when he smiled, and his eyes became narrow slits. He reminded me of a telephone pole, solid, seemingly unbreakable.

His pain resonated with me. I had not lost my mother the way Chip had lost Irene, but I knew loss, I had felt that emptiness. My younger brother Michael John's drowning days before his nineteenth birthday was a loss we both understood and formed a bond between us.

We were the siblings the furthest apart in age—almost eight years—but I felt a special connection to Chip almost immediately. While Tony and I were pals, brothers with a twist ... not rivals, but with a crosscurrent of healthy respect, Chip and I seemed comfortable with each other right from the start. He was quiet, composed, contained. He was methodical and deliberate, but not cold. He often hid his emotions, but some of the time, I could see through his stoical mask, even over the telephone. Chip did not back up or lean away. He stood there and let me in, like the way he came right out and told me about being in therapy after Irene died.

The word spontaneity did not spring to mind in the same sentence with Chip's name. This contributed to his solidness, a palpable feeling I had that when I was talking with Chip, I could count on things not changing. He was a creature of habit and in my mind, that said to me that he was a man I could rely on. While Tony often found humor in the world around him, Chip was quiet, letting his body speak when he had little to say. He fidgeted if he was not at least on his way to lunch at 11:30 a.m. He did not have to be eating by this time, but his body knew when it was pointed in the direction of food.

He may have been a Baby Boomer like his brothers and me, but Chip's disposition reminded me of my father's era: the

Greatest Generation. Dad had served in the Army in World War II and was comfortable saying little or nothing when others were in conversation around him. This described Chip, who can tell a story when you ask him. But you had to ask him, and if he had nothing to say he would not say anything. He was soft-spoken. His emotions emerged in his voice and the words he chose, more often than on his face. He had to hear something startling—a joke, a disagreeable argument, a wrong-headed suggestion— before he became animated. He'd lurch back in his chair and raise his eyebrows. He might wait two beats, and then his words would match the body language, like the flash of lightning that waits a moment for the soft clap of thunder to catch up.

He knew his way around a firearm and owned many. It might not be a good idea to be in Chip's presence if he ever became provoked. His demeanor hid a steeliness. They told me it was a McCrackin family trait to always want the last word. Taken to its extreme, especially when they were younger, the McCrackin boys often came to fisticuffs and were glad of a nurse for a mother.

Chip told me about a time when he was eight. "I was so angry at (middle brother) John, I loaded Daddy's shotgun and wanted to shoot him."

Chip never explained what the precipitating factor was, but who remembers what they were thinking at that age, or even, often, in a fit of rage?

Thankfully, Chip chose the incorrect shell for the gun in hand. "It slipped right through the barrel," he said. And out of harm's way.

Chip spoke obliquely about a childhood and youth that careened back and forth between civility and almost crossing the line into lawlessness. A Nichols police officer took Chip under his wing, as he told it, and set him on the right path.

Something stuck. As an adult, Chip became a law enforcement officer and graduated second in his class at the academy where he trained. A few years later, he transitioned into firefighting, first for Horry County as a volunteer. Then the county decided it needed a full-time fire department. Chip signed on, although he worked with a friend part-time building homes. But the professionalism of his police training, something he cherished and satisfied his natural inclinations, vanished, he told me, when he became a firefighter.

"I loved the discipline," he said of his police academy days. "I just soaked up the information. But the fire department was different. We learned from other volunteers. They kept telling me, 'This is all you need to know.' Well, I wanted to know more."

He and some of his like-minded colleagues coined a phrase: "Don't teach me the tricks of the trade. Teach me the trade."

He found a natural home when he accepted a new job with the North Myrtle Beach Fire Department. The position also came with mandatory training. Here, Chip discovered a real love. He committed for twelve years until the internal politics turned toxic. He was a lieutenant with leadership responsibilities, but he butted heads with the police commander who, oddly, managed both North Myrtle Beach's police and fire departments.

Chip needed no crystal ball. He quit, he said, before he knew he would have been fired.

"It was the best thing to happen to me," he said.

In a leap of faith—wasn't that how it usually happened?—his side gig as a house builder blossomed into full-time work as a contractor. For himself.

"It was the scariest thing I've ever done."

Today, his customers wait at least two years before he can get to their project. Occasionally he'll make an exception.

"The ones who yell the loudest," he says, deadpan.

"You mean like the squeaky wheel thing?" I asked.

"That's right."

Susan told me at least three times in phone chats that I had to ask Chip about the last time he lost his temper. It seemed to me that a man who had been in law enforcement for as many years as Chip had probably had many an opportunity to let it rip.

"Anyone who loses their temper should not be a law enforcement officer," he said. If wishing made it so.

So, when was the last time he lost his temper?

"Back in 1989," he said.

"Thirty years ago?"

"Uh-huh."

"What happened?"

He fought a tug-of-war with a piece of wire the diameter of his thumb, called an entrance wire. It runs from the meter base at the street to the main electric panel. He was rehabbing his first house just after he had married. This entrance wire put up a monster fight. It would not cooperate with him as he tried to snake it up a wall and down another in his attempt to connect it to the home's electric panel.

Here is how he tells it.

"I lost my temper. So then I laid down on my back, put my feet up against the wall and pulled that wire with everything I had. It gave."

"What did you mean," I asked, "when you said, 'I lost my temper'?"

"I don't recall," he said, again deadpan. "I'm sure I had a few choice words for that wire. I paid dearly. I pulled every muscle in my body. I didn't get out of bed for two days. I was sore for two weeks."

He coined a phrase, one I like a lot.

"I lost my temper, and I never found it," he said. "I'm a patient man."

Deadpan.

I expected to find myself in a foreign world, only to be surprised and relieved to be among people who were far more like me than not. Like me in more than in appearance and a few ingrained habits. I was spooked by our shared values, our common morals. Our politics were different, our cultural experiences were different, but these were insignificant.

As brothers, we—all three of us—also shared a vulnerability.

We each walked this earth with wounds that shaped us. Yet I sensed no self-pity in either man. We were like many other men. What made this experience new for me, and significant, was that these men were blood kin. When I peered into Chip's and Tony's eyes, I was looking into a mirror, and I saw familiar emotions I thought were unique only to me. Now, standing between them it brought me into not only a chronological alignment, but also a spiritual one I was only beginning to appreciate. It was as if we were jigsaw puzzle pieces that came together finally, after having been scattered across the floor, decades before finding one another.

My search was not necessary, but now that I had found the pieces, I felt content. It was like opening a keep-sake box you hadn't rummaged through in a while, not looking for anything, but coming across an old ribbon or coin and suddenly recalling a long-forgotten event. That's not quite it, but it's close. There was no perfect analogy. And that was acceptable.

At my first McCrackin family reunion in June 2018, Chip invited me to his home a couple miles from Tony and Marianne's place for a little fishing. He picked me up at Tony and Marianne's. On the way to his place, we stopped at a bait shop and bought a tin can's worth of live crickets and some earthworms. By the time we pulled into his driveway, the weather had begun to change. A light gray sky closed in on us and a flash of lightning lit up far off to the west. A clap of thunder hit our ears many seconds later. It was an approaching summer storm, but a slow-moving one and distant.

On the drive that hot and humid Saturday afternoon, Chip and I shared some comfortable brotherly silence, mixed with some small talk. Chip lives on a quiet stretch of Duford Road in Nichols. Everything in and around Nichols was a quiet stretch seen through my urban-colored glasses. Quiet to an LA boy and quiet to a Nichols boy were probably two different experiences. Here, in the middle of cotton and tobacco country, I heard no police sirens or helicopters, a ubiquitous soundtrack where I lived.

To Chip, his small piece of land was the essence of serene isolation. He owned a few acres that ran from the road back to a line of trees. The only other discernible boundary was the chest-high wall of corn to the north. It cut a severe path from the trees to the road as if it were a dark green fence. By late summer the corn would reach another two feet higher.

We were two brothers getting to know one another in person, which is different from talking on the phone. Late in the afternoon after the family reunion broke up, Chip and I gravitated to the pond he designed, dug, and filled on his property and which was a clear badge of pride. Chip loved sunsets and never tired of texting me new shots from his phone. He'd sunk pilings deep into the bottom of the pond about twenty feet from its edge and built a covered gazebo that sat on top of these pilings. The gazebo was connected to the pond's shore by a wood pier. Chip took every sunset photo he texted me while standing on the covered gazebo.

Chip suggested I start with the crickets since that is what his bass preferred. The tin can we'd bought was open-topped, a bit wider than a coffee tin, so I reached in and pincered one of the critters. It was soft and crinkly, squirmy, and pliant. Perhaps it knew its fate.

The hook penetrated easily, causing some of its innards to ooze. It was not all that different from an earthworm. A cricket is small, whereas an earthworm ... well, it is not unlike threading a needle, except you keep plunging the hook deeper and deeper into the worm until the hook no longer looks like a hook. You end up with a J-shaped worm dangling from the end of the fishing line.

Then into the water it went. The cricket, that is. The wait was short, a few seconds. The prize for each of us was a half-pound bass at best, and we threw them back immediately.

We heard thunder and when it was insistent, a flash or two of lightning turned our heads. But I was distracted with my fishing and didn't notice right away that the once-distant summer storm was marching toward us. Chip was used to this, but I lived in a desert. What others would call drizzle, we call rain in Los Angeles, and many of us don't know how to navigate even a little water on the roads.

Midwest weather, recalled from my boyhood days, can be biblical. Horizontal rain, winds that bend thick trees parallel to the ground, skies so dark at 10 a.m. it felt like evening, golf-ball-sized hail, lightning that split tree branches, thunder as loud as a bomb explosion (and I have never heard a bomb outside a Dolby-rigged movie theater). And once, many years ago, a tornado. But no locusts.

This summer storm was, instead, a quiet affair, with dark, fast-moving clouds and intense, blustery winds, but without threatening to knock anything to the ground and carry it off. Chip and I pulled in our lines and stowed the gear and bait. Then we stood in the center of the covered gazebo.

We watched the unfolding real-time special effects, more Disney than James Cameron. As we stood within the gazebo, we faced north and slightly west as the wind and rain came at us. Sometimes the wind swirled, and the rain darted directly toward us, as if it knew we were watching and wanted to show off its natural talents. We admired. The wind, the rain, the thunder all grew louder. Pebble-sized drops pelted the gazebo's roof like a thousand feet scrambling across it.

Like a quick inhale, the storm wandered off, over our covered heads, then past, farther off to the south and east. We turned slowly, following the mobile cacophony. A bright percussion of rain tickled the pond's still water, and a pale lightning flash overhead threw Chip and me into deep shadows from the gazebo. Not silence, but quiet resumed, like a lawn sprinkler that had been moved to a different part of the property.

The ground between the wood pier and the back door of Chip's house was now saturated. It was not lawn exactly. Nothing on his land fit that description. It was mud slush. We peeled off our shoes and socks, tucked them beneath our arms, and tip-toe-ran from the edge of the pier to the garage. The watery tracks were cold despite the warm air. We reached the back door and Chip entered to grab dry towels.

A few hours of fishing with my youngest brother as a summer storm visited was almost like a set piece in a novel. Chip joyously admitted that my presence provoked his memories, as if I were a production assistant who stood off-stage and prompted him when he forgot his lines. Chip found long-buried recollections of his childhood and about Irene.

Had I met this man in line at a grocery store checkout, I might have exchanged a few words. Small talk. Friendly, neighborly banter. Not much more. It is unlikely I would have chosen Chip to be my friend. He may think the same if the question were put to him.

He is now family. He is a blood brother, kin. We spent an afternoon saying not a hell of a lot, fishing, watching nature do what it does best, being brothers, the way brothers are when they're together.

Nothing required me to bond with Chip or Tony or Susan, with any of these good people. Nothing said I had to make them part of my life or keep them in my life. I could easily have made their acquaintance and let them go.

I could have walked away. I would not be the first adoptee who discovered lost family, only to draw a line and never cross it again. But that was not me. Nor was it Chip. Or Tony. Or Susan. The miracle was not that I overcame the obstacles I almost allowed to stop me from searching for my birth family.

The miracle was that I was embraced so effortlessly, without hesitation.

No, that was not a miracle. Not at all.

## 45

As if the infant bracelet Susan had given to me when we met for dinner in Reston, Virginia, in September 2017, was not an emotional shock, Susan dropped another bombshell on me that night. She told me that my birth father, Berlon, had been arrested, tried, convicted, and served time in prison.

"For murder," she said.

Susan divulged the short version of the story after dessert, enough to satisfy my curiosity and, I'm guessing, to reset my stunned face back to something resembling normal.

A few days later, after I returned to Los Angeles, I called her to ask more questions.

"I shouldn't have told you," she fretted. "It was too much too soon."

"No, I'm glad you did," I said. "The news was both a shock and a little entertaining."

I didn't want to offend my new sister, but the storyteller in me reveled in the news. Who doesn't get a bit giddy with family drama like that? Susan couldn't offer much more in terms of detail than she had revealed to me at dinner in Virginia.

That changed when I came to Nichols the last time, in

December 2019. Tony, his wife Marianne, Susan, Jayne, Chip, and I were sprawled across every piece of living-room furniture in Tony and Marianne's home, where I was again a guest. We had gorged at a favorite BBQ eatery and were collapsed and fighting a food coma. I thought it seemed like an opportune moment to ask about Berlon's felony conviction.

"Here," said Tony, handing me an aged, stained, and yellowed document that he'd retrieved from a file cabinet.

It was an official-looking pamphlet, about sixteen pages with two staples, labeled The State of South Carolina In The Supreme Court.

"What's this?" I said, staring at it.

"You can keep that," he said. "I have another copy."

"Is that the appeal?" Susan asked.

"Yes."

"Daddy never got a fair trial...," said Chip.

"...Well, he didn't have the sharpest lawyer," Jayne interrupted.

"That's a fact," Chip concurred.

"So what happened?" I asked.

"Daddy was accused of killing two girls," said Chip.

"But he wasn't even driving the car that hit them," Susan interjected.

"And Mayo wouldn't hire the lawyer Daddy wanted," said Tony, referring to his grandfather, Berlon's father.

I felt like a pinball, bouncing from one bumper to another, without getting anywhere or understanding anything.

"Wait," I said. "I'm not following you."

None of my siblings was even alive when Berlon was arrested for reckless homicide in October 1946. He hadn't even met Irene at this point in his life. In fact, the document Tony had given me, and the story I was about to hear, was more than seventy years gone. At the time, Berlon hadn't been old enough to drink or vote.

The account of Berlon's manslaughter charges and conviction

was not pieced together by family recollection. The evidence was documented, witnesses called, testimony recorded. I would read the appeals document later, many times, but as I sat in Tony and Marianne's living room on this night, I let my siblings tell me what they knew.

"Daddy was driving a Jeep and his friend, Howard, was in a Ford." Chip got the narrative started.

The two young men, both about nineteen, were driving on Nichols Highway outside Mullins, South Carolina, a paved, two-lane road with gravel shoulders. Howard Conner was at the wheel of the Ford. Berlon drove the Jeep.

"A drag race is what it was," said Chip.

A contest, a test of nerves, of courage, of masculinity. An adolescent rite of passage. The two vehicles sped east on Nichols Highway. But the cars were not in tandem. They were side by side.

This was a race. Howard's Ford was on the left, in the oncoming lane, where it was not supposed to be. Berlon's Jeep was in the right-hand lane, racing his friend and rival Howard.

No one knows who was ahead, who was behind, who caught up, who passed whom, or even how far down Nichols Highway the contest proceeded. They drove and drove, Howard looking to his right, Berlon to his left. They eyed one another to gauge each other's position. They were not paying attention to what was in front of them. They were in the moment. They were driving, but not navigating. They were steering but did not know where they were going.

Berlon and Howard failed to see the two girls or the motorized bicycle the girls were riding. They did not see the two lives approaching, growing larger in the windshields of their cars.

They did not see the enormity of the mark they and the families of the girls would carry forever. "There is no present or future, only the past," Eugene O'Neill wrote in *A Moon for the Misbegotten*, "happening over and over again, now." This was Berlon's indelible past.

The Ford and the Jeep hurtled down Nichols Highway, going nowhere, until the collision.

The girls died instantly.

The nearest witness was four-hundred feet away, according to the appeal brief. Howard's Ford left skid marks. Berlon's Jeep never stopped.

Howard's Ford struck the girls. Berlon's Jeep drove on until he arrived at his home, parked the vehicle, and went inside. Only later, when the police arrived to inform him of the fatalities did Berlon realize something had happened. So he said in his statement.

Howard Conner and Berlon McCrackin were charged. Howard's case was dismissed.

"He had a competent lawyer," said Susan. My siblings also believed Howard Conner had family connections. He had means. The appeal brief, not surprisingly, explained none of this.

Berlon's charges were not dropped. He went to trial. He was convicted. He served eighteen months. His appeal was filed with the South Carolina Supreme Court. He claimed that as the driver of the Jeep, he never struck the two girls on their motor bicycle. All the evidence pointed to Howard Conner and his Ford. The skid marks. The paint left on the bicycle that matched the Ford.

The handful of eyewitnesses, even the ones who were far from the accident scene, pointed at Berlon. Not Howard.

Bad boy Berlon. Whose reputation may very well have sauntered into the courtroom long before he did. His appeal was denied.


MY SIBLINGS SMILED and laughed out loud at my confusion as we lay around Tony and Marianne's living room.

"It's a complicated story," said Tony.

"We still get riled up about it," added Jayne, without an ounce of irritation in her voice. In fact, I didn't hear any rancor as my new brothers and sisters unraveled the plot of this family saga.

Whatever they had experienced had been left on the roadside years ago.

Tony said the story was complicated. It seemed straightforward to me. Howard Conner got off when he should have been convicted if I understood the facts correctly. But Berlon was not innocent. He was complicit even if he wasn't directly responsible. He chose to drive recklessly in a way that resulted in the deaths of two girls.

In a small town like Mullins, South Carolina, everyone knew everyone—the oldest fact of life in small-town and rural America. Earn a reputation and the lens becomes a microscope. When the reputation reeks of malice, the microscope adds heat.

My siblings argued that because Berlon could not afford adequate representation, he received an unfair trial. The appeal brief submitted to the South Carolina Supreme Court was written by his lawyer, even though it was not the lawyer Berlon asked for, so of course its narrative is biased in Berlon's favor. I wondered if Berlon's reputation did more to convict him than anything that transpired on Nichols Highway.

I had to go back as far as my high school days to recall a boy who had a reputation anything like Berlon's. A reputation that scared me. A reputation that caused me to turn around and walk in a different direction at the sight of him.

An ex-con was not the man, the entire man, my birth siblings grew up with, lived with, and loved. I may not have had skin in the game, and in the company of my birth siblings, drowsy and relaxed by the rich meal we had just shared, I may also have been gripped slightly by the bias I felt in the air, but I found myself unperturbed by their tale. I sympathized with my siblings' doubts about Berlon's turn in the justice system. No one should be defined only by their actions or behavior as a young person, and Berlon had paid both the price and his debt.

## 46

A phrase stood out from the note Dad gave me in the 1980s describing my birth father. It is odd and doesn't explain much to me. The phrase, written in my Dad's neat handwriting, was "gentleman farmer."

What it meant escaped me. He was a farmer, but apparently more than your average farmer. I didn't get the "gentleman" part.

Dad said it meant he did not farm his land himself, but instead let others do that for him and paid him for the privilege. So, I concluded, my birth father was also clever, an entrepreneur. When my buddies in elementary school asked me what a gentleman farmer was, I kept my answer simple, but I knew I liked him in a way you like someone based only on a glancing first impression.

Later, of course, I would learn that a gentleman farmer, by definition, is a rich farm owner who farms as a hobby, not for a living. And after I met my birth siblings, I discovered that Dad's definition did not match reality. Berlon was not a "gentleman farmer."

The picture Irene painted of Berlon in the adoption report hardly squared with the real-life portrait my birth siblings and birth-family members described. The only and obvious rationale is clear to anyone who wishes to see it: Irene loved him. When questioned by the social worker in Milwaukee as she tells her story running up to the delivery of her illegitimate child (me), Irene fibbed about Berlon's height, his education, his build.

He never finished high school. Only a woman in love would see a V-shaped superman. This was also part of a story she wanted the would-be adoptive couple to know.

On each of my visits to Nichols, I slept in what used to be Berlon and Irene's bedroom and saw what appeared to be a surveyor's map on the wall next to their bed. It was a detailed map of the McCrackin family farm in its heyday.

The map was a reimagining of the farm and had been drawn in the 2000s. It showed two plots of land, one on each side of the highway that divided their property. They totaled forty-six acres, a few acres smaller than the original farm, the bulk of the land on the west side of the two-lane "highway." Another road began its life at this highway, not a hundred feet from the McCrackin family house, and stretched out east and a little south, a half a mile before dying abruptly at a shallow ditch. This meager pavement served as the southern property line.

Berlon was not a man of means, but he was a man of opportunity. When the pig business he had started years earlier faltered, he had another plan. He was a fair man who wanted to help his neighbors while also providing his family with extra income. He succeeded at both. He had small parcels of the farm, originally about fifty-four acres, surveyed and divided into tracts of one and two acres, give or take. These he offered to local folks who had no credit or poor credit, for a given period at an affordable monthly payment. Sometimes for a year, sometimes longer, until they'd built up the equivalent of a down payment. Then he would vouch for these lessors when they applied for a mortgage at a local bank.

Berlon charged a higher interest than a bank, but then he was taking a bigger risk. He sold off six tracts of land this way, helping a few neighbors while he pocketed a nice, but not excessive, profit for himself and his family. He had the spirit of an entrepreneur.

. . .

The farm was also home to horses, although from the way my new siblings described things, Berlon was more comfortable around pigs.

One of the horses kept by the McCrackins was named Tammy, an American Saddle Horse whom Susan loved to ride. One day, Berlon was cleaning out Tammy's stall in the barn. He had tied her to a railing outside the stall. Apparently, Tammy did something Berlon did not like and from the story that emerged, Tammy and Berlon faced off. The horse let Berlon know exactly how she felt about him.

"I didn't see what happened," explained Chip, who was in the barn's tackle room at the time and only heard the ruckus. "But it was clear to me that Tammy tried to kick Daddy. He was having none of it."

Berlon went after Tammy with a three-tined pitchfork.

"I looked out the tackle room door," said Chip, "and I saw Daddy chasing Tammy. He got her into her stall, but she was mad, let me tell you."

Mad, yes, but cornered.

"I just stayed put," said Chip. "But I could see everything. Tammy tried to get around Daddy, but he jabbed her with the pitchfork. He didn't break the skin, just let her know who was boss."

Chip, who was in high school at the time, swore the story was gospel.

"I guess Tammy'd had enough," said Chip, "because she got down on her front knees in the stall like she was bowing to him. I saw it with my own eyes."

Tammy never tried to kick him again.

Berlon McCrackin, horse whisperer. With the aid of a pitchfork.

. . .

TODAY, the house sits proudly on a rise just where the highway dips and curves around a small creek on its way north. Only memories, old photos and the surveyor's map on Berlon and Irene's bedroom wall remain of the original farm.

Every photo in their bedroom was at least fifty years old. Irene's landscapes and bird drawings were a few years younger. A black and white photo of a slender Berlon in his Korean War Army uniform sat on a dresser opposite the bed. In it, he is smiling. His pomaded dark hair shows off a couple strands curled over his forehead as if he were a movie actor, sitting for a movie-poster headshot.

In the room where the man had slept, woke, dressed, lived, his sepia visage conveyed hope twinged with mischievousness. It was taken at a time when he was closer to his bad-boy days than he was to being a father, when life for him was all fourth gear. I was not even a thought in his head. I studied those dark, searching eyes and saw myself as if I were gazing into a mirror.

This was my birth father, the man who lay with Irene and ignited my life.

He was my blood kin. Were he alive today and we stood shoulder to shoulder, no one would have doubted that we were father and son. The resemblance was unambiguous.

I have slept in the bedroom Berlon and Irene shared. I saw and felt their presence in the objects they owned, lived with, played on. I slept soundly in their bed. Yet they did not speak to me in the night.

Each morning I woke to the muffled sounds of Marianne in her kitchen across the hall from where I slept, and the aroma of coffee and bacon sizzling in the fry pan. The north-facing room stayed dark even after the sun rose. Flat on my back, I gazed up at Berlon's guitar and Tony's banjo and the map of the farm on the wall to my left.

What would it have been like to live here as a boy? To grow up here? To have two older sisters and three younger brothers? That was not the life I lived. And while I wondered about it from time to time, the thought did not linger.

I had grown up somewhere else with different siblings, in a different setting, in a place where I felt and was made to feel whole and complete. Mom and Dad did the right things for me and Jo and whatever that was, my yearning to know about my birth mother fled, as if Dumbledore had extracted the memory of her with his wand and deposited it in a Pensieve for someone else to relive. She was not my memory.

Lying here surrounded by momentos of the lives of my birth mother and birth father did not stir me to pangs of longing. This was not the room where I was conceived, but then I was not an afterthought in this room either. It is probable that Irene had recurring dreams about me right here. And that Berlon might have wondered, in the night, what his first son, whom he'd never seen, looked like, sounded like.

This room welcomed me back often. Tony and Marianne will invite me again to be their guest, and I will return as their brother, as family. But it is not my home.

## 47

I rene had a reputation for independence, for standing her ground. She could take care of herself. Many members of my birth family were eager to share an anecdote about Irene to corroborate this side of her. One came from my new Aunt Johann, a small, gregarious woman with a gift for conversation. There was no such thing as a short phone call with Aunt Johann. She is the widow of my late Uncle Windell McCrackin, my birth father's youngest brother, who was in his late eighties when I met him on my first trip to Nichols. He died in 2020 at ninety, a year after my last visit.

Aunt Johann told me that when Irene and Berlon were first married, they moved in with Berlon's parents, John Mayo, whom everyone called Mayo, and Donnie, or Miss Donnie. Mayo was gruff. Aunt Johann suspects that he physically abused Berlon as a child. Mayo apparently accepted Irene, but she was not from the South. She was tolerated. Irene, according to Aunt Johann, tolerated the toleration. But when Mayo crossed a line, as he did one evening at the dinner table, Irene showed her metal. She threatened him with a knife.

The full story was one of many that emerged on my visits to Nichols. When my siblings and I gathered in Tony and Marianne's living room after dinner, the mood was set for easy, uninhibited talk.

"You remember what that was all about?" asked Susan as Jayne, Tony, Marianne, Chip, and I settled ourselves in chairs or on the sofa. The flat-screen television attached to a wall was on with the volume turned off.

"Heck, that was before we were born," said Chip, producing a chorus of laughter.

"But Daddy told you a lot of his stories, didn't he?" asked Tony.

"Sure, he did," said Chip. "I think Mayo just accused Momma of threatening him."

"How do you mean?" I asked.

"There was tension between her and Mayo," he said, "but I don't think Momma was serious. I think she got angry at him about something and had a knife in her hand as they were eating."

"And Mayo accused her of threatening him?" asked Susan.

"Something like that," said Chip.

Threat or no threat, I'm willing to bet it was not the butter knife.


IRENE OWNED a Winchester Boy's rifle, a small twenty-two caliber. She used it to shoot cowbirds, a species that threatened the local songbirds she adored. Cowbirds would lay their eggs in the songbird nests, and when they hatched, they'd push out the songbird chicks.

One day, at the house in Nichols, where she and Berlon raised their five children, she carried the rifle outside where some men were working in the yard. They razzed her about the gun, playfully but relentlessly claiming she did not know how to use it. This story came from Chip.

"Care to show me how?" she asked her inquisitors.

One of them took the bait. She handed the rifle to the volunteer, then walked to a fence post about a hundred feet away and set up an old soda can. The man took aim, fired off three shots and hit the can once.

Irene smiled at him and his smug companions. As Chip told it, Irene kneeled and picked up the empty .22 casings, walked to the fence and pushed one of the empties into the post with her bare hand. Her unwitting chorus of detractors was perplexed when she rejoined them. She picked up the rifle, loaded it and took aim. She fired three times. Each shot, according to Chip, drove the pushed-in empty casing farther into the fence post.

The men, their egos thoroughly deflated, stood frozen, disbelief in their eyes. Irene had made her point.

Not bad for a Milwaukee transplant to the Deep South.


I HAD to accept that so many questions I wanted to ask about Irene would go unanswered. The simplest, most basic questions, like: how did she travel from South Carolina back to Milwaukee, pregnant with me, along with two-year-old Susan and eighteen-month-old Jayne? In 1956, I doubt she flew on an airplane. Her husband Junior had been killed in his car, which was totaled by the sound of things from his obituary, probably leaving Irene without transportation. More likely, she took a Greyhound bus.

But it's all idle speculation. Irene managed as she always seemed to manage after returning to Milwaukee to have me, to deal with me, to extricate herself from me. She had to do that first. One thing at a time. One foot after the other. She came back to Mullins planning to leave it. Instead, she stayed to start her life over and build a family with Berlon.

Mt. Sinai Hospital, in Milwaukee, was Irene's home twice in her life. She did her nurse training there in the 1940s before she joined the Army. It was also where she gave birth to me. It was not a coincidence. It was her plan. To escape the small-town claustrophobia of Mullins and her late husband's family, she traveled north to be with her own family. My adoption report does not say so in direct language, but you can deduce that she came back to familiar territory.

Linda and I talked about this part of the adoption report, speculating on what Irene might have been thinking.

"My guess," said Linda, "is that she still knew someone at Mt. Sinai. Someone she trusted."

"A nurse?" I said.

"Possibly. But she needed a doctor, a man, to help her."

A man? Yes, a man. A doctor was a man in Milwaukee in the 1950s, almost without exception. A man as an ally, Linda said, would give her the cover she needed. It grated on my twenty-first century ears, but this was the reality.

Linda thought she likely chose one of the staff physicians to help her create a cover story when it was time for her to deliver me. Linda and I agreed that Irene was industrious, resilient, brave.

My birth siblings have endured my queries about their mother, my birth mother, probably to annoyance. They know more about her than anyone alive, but when you press someone for a detail, a story, a telling anecdote, the result is usually a blank, an empty well. These kinds of stories bubble up in the context of a conversation, sparked by a sudden remembrance, a connection that can't be forced. When I played the role of a television interviewer, I did not get the desired insights.

Instead, the stories emerged in car rides, after a meal, walking around the farm. They didn't form a whole picture, and I wonder now if that was a false hope. I know almost as much about Irene from the picture that developed from my adoption report as I learned from the bits and pieces of stories I've collected from Susan, Jayne, Tony, Chip.

Who could describe their mother or father definitively in a single story? Or twenty-seven stories? Short of writing a biography, the task was virtually impossible. Biographers will say that a biography is not a life. It is, at best, a collection of anecdotes and scraps of memories, assembled astutely, which was the biographer's job—the historian Shelby Foote called biographers "pick-locks"—into a whole that delivered the impression of a life.

Irene remained two-dimensional. I have photographs, most of them black and white, the color images having faded, from the 1950s, '60s and '70s. They were two generations old. All her children said a variation of the same thing: Irene did not like to have her picture taken. Predictably, there were few. That she died at forty-six meant the opportunity to capture her on film was about half the typical lifespan.

What I had learned barely added up to a shadow of a life. But I was hardly distraught and not sad. The image of a jigsaw puzzle on a card table returned to me, with only a few of the pieces connected. I would be lost in the wilderness of these pieces for a long time with no guarantee of understanding their whole.

It was enough.

## 48

A five-year wait for vindication is a long time. Five years to stumble across someone to rebut Nancy Verrier. I had accepted with equanimity that adoption was a traumatic experience and that I had suffered scars from the event that happened long before I was ever conscious of it. But I had not been defined by those scars and I believed I had overcome their effects. How and by what mechanisms, I did not know with certainty. Mom and Dad had done something, probably many things, right. What were they?

And then I made a discovery that changed everything.

I reread a familiar passage in Verrier's first book, *The Primal Wound*, and this triggered anew my research appetite. The precipitating words vibrated in my skull. Verrier pulled no punches in her books. She spoke in sweeping, declarative sentences, and here, as I remembered reading, was the linchpin of her argument:

"Babies should never be separated from their mothers unless it is absolutely necessary," she wrote, "because separation causes trauma, and trauma leaves the child wounded. The wound affects adoptees all their lives and greatly impacts their relationships with others as they go through the life cycle [...] Yet one of the residues of abandonment is a perpetual feeling of being a victim, of being powerless, of being helpless to help oneself."

But who out there in the world of adoption research would challenge her Primal Wound Theory? I wanted a counterargument from a clinical expert to corroborate my experience. I went online again and searched Verrier's name and a few keywords. I'd done this countless times. Why was I bothering now, long after I'd received my adoption report, long after my many visits to South Carolina and countless texts, Zoom, and phone calls? Long after I had satisfied myself that she was mistaken?

Unrelenting tenacity. I held fast to the fundamental truth of my lived experience. But subjective truth was not enough. I also leaned into my scientific literacy, that I could read closely and dissect a weak argument when I encountered it. In my opinion and experience, Nancy Verrier's arguments failed to describe me. And lots of other adoptees like me.

My internet search produced links that took me to familiar blog posts, scholarly articles, book reviews. The exercise was routine, what any researcher does, but so often the effort was repetitive or fruitless.

This search, however, produced something new. After examining one more link and reading the few words visible, I hesitated. It appeared to be something I'd seen before.

"Check the source, Howard," I said to myself. "Don't dismiss what you haven't explored." I clicked through to a video on YouTube and my jaw dropped open. I'll never forget the date: November 7, 2020, three and a half years after I finished reading Verrier's textbooks.

This was something entirely different. I had not watched this video before and did not recognize the people on the screen capture. I squinted and stared into this new and unfamiliar face.

He was wearing a dark suit and reddish horn-rimmed glasses that framed his sad eyes in round lenses. His prominent nose poked out from within a white beard that flowed down to his chest and hid the top half of his red-striped tie. His shiny forehead reflected a bright overhead light. His name was Michael Grand.

The interviewer, an adoption therapist and adoptee, sat to the left of Grand. She described Verrier's *The Primal Wound*, how the book spoke to her and other adoptees. "Somebody understands me and finally knows who I am," she said of Verrier. "And it becomes the adoptee bible."

Well, I'd heard this all before. I almost clicked the back button, but something stilled my hand. The interviewer, Jeanette Yoffe, MA, MFT, repeated the story I had rejected. I cringed and pushed my chair away from my desk, away from this new person. I found myself talking back to a grainy color image on a computer monitor. Where were the cute kitten videos when I needed them?

But I was not clicking away.

Why was I not clicking away?

Something held me in place.

Yoffe said that her guest's book, *The Adoption Constellation*, presented a different perspective on the Primal Wound Theory.

She asked Grand to explain his thinking.

"Nancy Verrier's book," he began in his slow, deliberate cadence, "captures for some adoptees the experience of pain and grief and loss that so many others have denied to them. And in that sense, it's a very important and moving book."

Wait. Did he say, "...for *some* adoptees..."?

Grand had my attention. I pulled my chair closer to the desk and leaned into the monitor.

"Having said that," he continued, "Verrier's explanation of that experience and the ways to move forward from that position (of pain and grief) are flawed."

Oh my God. He challenged the accepted wisdom of Verrier.

"I think at the heart of a successful adoption," he said, "is that we treat each other in a way that we have mutual mattering between us."

Mattering. I knew the word, but I had never heard it used in this context before. It was so simple: when a parent demonstrates to a child that the child is important to the parent in every way, and then expresses gratitude when the child returns the feeling.

Labeling an adoptee as a victim of trauma, said Grand, creates a self-fulfilling prophecy. Adoptive parents who communicate to their adopted child that they matter to them is the key to breaking the mold of the victimhood of trauma. Mattering, said Grand, allows the adoptee to create a personal narrative in which the adoptee builds a sense of wholeness.

Mattering extends out beyond the adoptive mother and father, he said. It includes siblings, cousins, aunts and uncles, teachers, neighbors, religious leaders. And especially grand-parents.

If grandparents embrace the adopted child unconditionally, not as the "adopted" grandchild, but simply the *grandchild*, this defines Grand's *adoption constellation*, the title of his book.

Then he told a story about one of his patients, an adoptee, whose father demonstrated mattering. The adoptee loved sports and played on his high school football team, said Grand, but his adoptive father was a "klutz" and hated all sports.

"But my dad came to every game I played in," said the adoptee.

By this time, tears were running down my cheeks. I've rewatched this interview a few times and I still choke up at this point. My dad loved sports and he always came to watch me and my teammates play our games.

I wept because Michael Grand confirmed for me what I already knew but until this moment, I did not have the *vocabulary* to explain what I knew.

Mom and Dad showed me that I mattered. My grandparents embraced me unconditionally. My family constellation was broad and deep. These facts explain why I had never felt pain or grief about being an adoptee. I had no reason to.

My narrative started early in my life. I had the space. My adop-tion constellation *gave* me the space, to develop my own narrative.

I put my cursor on the video playback's red dot and slid it to the left many times.

Michael Grand brought me the words I'd longed for. He delivered them in the quiet but firm voice of a clinical psychologist who had earned his doctorate at the State University of New York at Stony Brook. Grand was an adoptee, too.

Though I had already concluded all this, Grand validated me. He gave me the counterargument to Verrier I craved. I stood up from my chair, fists raised as if my beloved Green Bay Packers had scored a touchdown.

In the span of one short video interview, I realized I had known more about myself as an adoptee than I ever gave myself credit for. As if I had been muted for sixty years, and now I could speak.

That afternoon, I bought *The Adoption Constellation* on Amazon and was royally peeved because I had to wait five days to receive it. My *Amazon Prime* membership, promising free two-day shipping, became sub-*Prime* and there was nothing I could do about it.

But when Grand's book arrived, I inhaled all two-hundred pages in an afternoon—funny how it took me two years to read Verrier—and the following morning, highlighting passages and tabbing pages as if I'd be quizzed on the material the next day.

There was no scientific evidence, Grand said, to support Verrier's explanation of the pain some adoptees experience. Two of Verrier's main arguments in her theory, that adoptees are unable to "attach" to their adoptive mothers, and that the Primal Wound is the "underlying cause of emotional and behavioral difficulties," he wrote, do not withstand scrutiny. I read similar words in Grand's text as he challenged Verrier's Primal Wound Theory. For example:

"...at least one is on firm ground to argue that there is nothing in the research on infant attachment behavior that would currently support Verrier's position," and

"The research evidence again proves otherwise" and

"If anything, these studies would suggest that the opposite

occurred" and

"Again, these results call into question the validity of the Primal Wound theory."

I have read countless articles on adoption, and three in-depth books on the subject. Two of those works were written by Nancy Verrier, one by Michael Grand. This makes me a well-read layperson, not an expert, but I found Grand's counterargument compelling.

Page after page after page, Grand cited research studies and papers. He questioned, poked holes in, and invalidated significant portions of Verrier's thinking. Her Primal Wound Theory, he wrote, "[...] is a psychologically deterministic theory. It posits that adoptees have no choice, and their life course is set at that moment after birth when they are physically removed from the birth mother. There is little that can be done to avoid the pain inflicted by the primal wound of separation or the resulting status of victim that shapes their future emotional relationships."

I wanted to scream, "See?! I told ya so!" at the top of my lungs.

But Nancy Verrier deserves her due. She did a thorough job of revealing the pain many adoptees feel. She conducted the first serious inquiry to ask those adoptees about their fears and feelings of anguish.

Michael Grand challenged how she arrived at her findings about the causes of that pain. A passage from Grand captured my attention and in an instant of clarity, revealed the core of my rejection of Verrier's victim-based approach:

"Validation of a theory," wrote Grand, "requires not only that there be empirical support for its hypotheses, but in addition, alternative explanations for the findings, other than those posed by the theory, *must be ruled out*. I believe that a careful reading of the clinical research literature will lead us to a very different understanding of the pain that Verrier documents so well." (Emphasis added.)

Verrier wasn't wrong about the anguish some adoptees experienced. She was wrong to claim that all adoptees experience the same anguish in the same way. She was wrong about me. And I believe other adoptees will find solace in learning this truth.

Grand showed me why I did not fit Verrier's profile and confirmed what I had believed but had struggled to articulate. And he went further. In clear prose, unlike so many academics, Grand said I was responsible for my own narrative, aided by the love and support of my family. My extended family.

Grand said that the difference between adoptees who felt victimized by pain and loss over the course of their lives and those who adapted and moved on from this anguish, rested on their personal narratives. All human beings create narratives for and about themselves, starting as children. Even and especially, Grand reminded me, the narratives adoptees construct.

The title of Grand's book, *The Adoption Constellation*, described my life as an adoptee, from infancy on. I was never made to feel that I had been an outsider joining someone else's family. I was never shamed for being an adoptee. I was never referred to or treated as a second-class son or brother or grandson. And in numerous ways, mostly non-verbal, my adoptive parents showed me that I "mattered," a key principle in Grand's thinking.

In other words, my family nurtured me so that I possessed the tools to navigate the messy aftermath of my adoption, an aftermath I did not know I needed or wanted to examine until much later in my life. I was not only *part of the Ibach family* on the day I arrived, but I was also the first member of Mom and Dad's brood. Their constellation began with me and became mine.

Well, not exactly day one. I came home with them when I was twenty-seven days old. On that day, I began forging the narrative of my life. A narrative, I am happy to report, that brooked no tolerance for victimhood.

I felt a weight fall from my shoulders. Vindicated at last. And then I laughed at myself. As if I needed evidence to believe what I believed. It helped, of course, but then I reminded myself that believing is seeing.

## 49

The last time I hugged Dad was so far in the past, I measure it in decades, two decades, and it was on a visit to Austin from my home in Los Angeles. I leaned in and he reached for my right hand. Dad did not reject my embrace, but when I stood back, he said calmly, "We don't need the hugging," a royal command in third person. Dad had never been comfortable with physical displays of affection. It was something I got used to and I never took this remoteness personally.

I was not thinking about that moment so many years earlier when I sat on the edge of Dad's hospital bed. We had moved him on September 1, 2022, to an assisted-living apartment in the secluded and wooded hills of Austin. I had moved here from Los Angeles fourteen months earlier because I wanted to be closer to family, and close to Dad.

He was placed on hospice care three weeks later, and the doctors told me, my sister Linda, and her husband Mike that Dad had only days to live. I sat with him on Thursday, September 29, and he was breathing heavily and to my eyes and ears and not least my heart, with difficulty. His eyes were closed and every few seconds he exhaled a loud sigh as if he were in pain. Yet I saw no constrictions in his ninety-six-year-old face or anywhere in his prone frame, so the sounds of his exhale contrasted with his visibly calm body. He was somewhere between awake and asleep, in a semi-comatose plateau.

Dad may not have liked that I sat so closely to him, but I did not care. Our time was short, and I wanted him to know in whatever way he might sense it, that I was there with him. So, I leaned in again, not to hug him but to let him feel me close by. It was about 3 pm and I held his right hand in my left hand, but I felt no grip. He did not return the gentle squeeze of my fingers. His hand was limp, but the skin was smooth and dry. My right had lain flat on his bony chest, fingers splayed.

"I love you, Dad," I said in a quiet voice, looking into his closed eyes. My right hand pressed gently into his chest through the navy sweatshirt the hospice nurses had dressed him in. He was breathing through his mouth, and he exhaled with another sigh, but this time, I heard a deep rasp.

"I love you," I repeated. Dad turned his head a little in my direction and opened his right eye. He fixed me with his single orb. We held that glance for a full ten seconds before he closed his eye.

I want to believe he knew me. I want to believe he saw how much I loved him. Although he was alive and breathing in this moment, I felt it was our parting.

My sister Linda had come into the room, but I did not hear her right away. I don't know how long she had been standing behind us as I sat with Dad, but when I heard movement behind me, her feet shuffling on the linoleum floor, the whisper of fabric, her breathing, I turned. Some sixth sense told me she had been watching us for a couple of seconds before she made her presence known. She was photographing me and Dad with her eyes and embedding the image of us deep into her heart, father and son at the end of a long, sublime adventure together.

My senses peaked on this day, as if the lights in the room had been turned up and I could see things in sharper relief. No premonition came to me about when Dad would die, but I knew it would be soon.

"Would you like to shave him?" Linda asked, rummaging in her shoulder bag, and handing me Dad's electric razor. I took it from her and for an instant I was transported back to Jonathan Lane in Bayside where, at the age of thirteen, I had sneaked into Mom and Dad's bathroom one morning before school and found Dad's Remington. I closed their bedroom door and then their bathroom door so no one could hear me, and I touched the quiet, vibrating smooth steel blades to my upper lip, whisking away the wispy peach fuzz for the first time. Now, fifty-two years later, I was about to shave Dad for the first time.

Dad's whiskers were as white as mine. I was an old man shaving a dying elderly man. I think he knew I was there because he turned his chin toward me. Five or six minutes later, Dad was clean shaven. As I beheld the face of the one human being who knew me longer and better than anyone on the planet—my father for sixty-five years and more than ten months—I realized that not since Dad had carried me as an infant and as a toddler grasped my hand as we walked together and tossed me in his arms and steadied me on my bicycle had we had as much physical contact as we did in the previous ninety minutes. Dad's imminent death broke down that barrier. Blessings sometimes come late and in unexpected ways.

At 4:30, I left Dad's room. Linda stayed with him until about eight that night. The next morning, I woke to a text waiting for me, a text I had not heard because I turned off my phone. It was from Linda, sent at 12:49 a.m. on Friday, September 30.

"Poppop died a little while ago," she wrote, using the name his grandchildren had given him. "The hospice people just called me."

IN LATE OCTOBER, I flew north to Milwaukee where I joined my family for Dad's funeral. The day before we buried him next to Mom, I drove from my hotel a few miles north toward Bayside and stopped for breakfast. As I parked my rental in front of the restaurant at an intersection of two streets whose names I knew as well as my own, the surroundings felt foreign, out of place. My heart was beating a little faster than normal as I pressed the "lock" button on my key and walked into the restaurant.

"Is this what it's like to go back in time?" I thought to myself. The businesses on every corner were new, the faces were new, but everything else appeared and felt so familiar. I half expected an old friend, perhaps a former neighbor, to meet me as I reached the restaurant door and say, "Well, hello, Howard!" Instead, I ate alone and in silence, paid my bill and drove the two miles up Port Washington Road to Orchard Highlands, the small subdivision where I grew up at the northern-most edge of Milwaukee County. But I was not there to revisit my boyhood home, although I would certainly see it. I had walked its rooms for the first time in decades in 2008 when I returned to Milwaukee to bury Mom.

Today I had other plans.

Not since I was sixteen years old, almost fifty years ago, had I descended into the ravine that surrounded the old family home on Jonathan Lane. This earthy, resinous space, an extension of the home I lived in by virtue of its familiar terrain, where my friends and I played cops and robbers, cowboys and Indians, nature boys on dangerous missions invented in our wild imaginings, was as real in my memories as the wrinkles on my face. Every day, many times a day, I thought about this ravine. Would it be anything like I remembered? How much would be different? How could I tell? Fifty years, half a century, is almost a lifetime, *is* a lifetime for some. An imposing tree I saw on a summer outing when I was eleven could now be toppled and rotting into the fertile soil.

None of that mattered. I was not returning to this place to visit a tree, not even many trees, perhaps most of them aged, dead or dying, and returning to their source, fertilizing a new generation of forest. I was home to perform an ancient ritual, a son burying his father, but first I wanted to visit the place where my life began, where my earliest memories took root. I wanted to climb down the steep slopes of the ravine, feel the wine-press layers of new and rotting leaves, fecund earth, and crunchy remains of branches beneath my feet, stand on the banks of the stream, and experience with my eyes, my ears, my nose, and my fingers what I had cherished and missed and dreamt about all these years. And to close my eyes and remember.

When I turned onto Jonathan Lane and allowed my car to ease its way down the cul-de-sac, the road bent rightward around a tall line of arbor vitae. Mom had planted these bushy, soft-focus versions of Christmas trees in the spring of 1959, only months after we had moved in the previous November. My boyhood home emerged from behind the evergreens as I maneuvered the car farther down the cul-de-sac. With the sun now topping the tallest trees to the east, the light that hit the structure's north-facing facade left it in a haze. Was my imagination playing tricks on me? Or was the house giving my memory a moment to catch up to its wood, stone, glass, and breathing dimensions?

A new stand of maturing trees fronted the property creating a theatrical effect, like woody lace curtains hiding the house from the street. They were not here when I visited in 2008. Even though I did not live here any longer, I found myself feeling protective of the house and its surroundings. I liked that passersby now had an obstructed view.

I slowed, pulled my car a few feet into the shallow grassy ditch in front of the house and stopped. I had mowed this yard count-less times over many summers as a boy and a teen. The woods surrounding the dead-end street surprised me because in late October, the colors were intense, yet the dense growth had thinned as summer gave way to fall and winter was making plans. Wisconsin painted a late morning with yellow and pale red and rust and nutmeg-colored leaves draped against a blue dome of sky to welcome me back to a neighborhood I knew so well. Memory and reality finally came into focus, as if I had taken off a pair of 3D glasses and a switch had flipped from dream-infused sight back to normal. Even sitting in my car, looking out its windows, this normal was an oxygen I had not breathed in decades.

I turned off the car's engine and sat. At 10:40 on a Friday morning, the air was still yet melodious with birdsong. I felt a deep churning in my gut as I stepped out of the car. I opened the back door, sat, and changed into my Wellingtons. Then I walked across the narrow lane, through the ditch and up to the ravine's edge. I peered down, as much into the past as into the ravine. My heart raced and my throat constricted.

The wooded canvas spread out before me was just as I remembered it, even if nothing was familiar. I thought to myself, I'm home.

The descent was steep, but not as treacherous as I feared. When you're twelve or fifteen, such a place is a jungle gym to be conquered. When you're sixty-five, it is a poorly lit basement strewn with long-forgotten belongings and twisted ankles lurking around every dark corner. Thankfully autumn pruned back the dense greenery, making navigation easier. I counted my blessings.

My Wellingtons were a wise choice. The ground beneath my feet was moist and spongy, but also noisy as I snapped twigs and sank a half-inch or more into the dank soil, my weight squeezing water and muddy earth into the shapes of treaded rubber soles. A thick, dark odor assaulted my nose and I had to think for a moment before I recalled that I had smelled it before. A long time ago. Here.

The stream was only a few paces from me, and I stopped well short. What I saw caught me off guard and was without a doubt different from what I had remembered. The banks of the stream were as tall as me, in some places over my head. A quick scan of my memory reminded me that decades of heavy snows and spring thaws and thunderstorms probably added up to a rush of water down what I remembered as a picturesque brook and turned it into a near-flooding onslaught of water. The ravine itself, and the surrounding neighborhoods, would never be in danger because its walls were prohibitively high, but five decades of weather speeds up geology. Weather changes what it touches. The foot-tall banks on both sides of the stream I knew in my boyhood had been carved into a micro-canyon within the ravine and I was stunned by the sight. A sinking feeling clutched at my stomach because this place, protected from the modern world, unpolluted still, the safe harbor of my memories, had been changed.

Summer had always been my favorite time to explore this space. The ravine's dense vegetation and the trees in full greenery dulled the high-walled environment to the hush of a church. But I was standing here in almost peak autumn, late October, surrounded by and atop color. I felt as if I were inside a painting but instead of brushstrokes of color, I stood on fragments of fallen red and brown and gold in the shapes of leaves, torn leaves, gray and darkly rotted twigs, and small branches separated from fallen trees, bits of black and dark brown earth, peeking up from the canvas I stood on. Beginnings and endings, the promise of new growth in the coming year, evidence of regeneration as huge fallen trees laid out across the stream and on the ravine, floor slowly decomposing to feed the soil.

For more than an hour I retraced my steps as a boy, but nothing sparked a recollection, no bend in the stream produced a story, until I found where the two bodies of water—the one I was following and the one that traversed the ravine behind my boyhood home—came together. And I found the flat, pebble-scattered wash where my best friend Cliff and I had made our discovery more than fifty-five years earlier.

This spot was so close to where I had parked my car, so close to the homes up the steep slopes that I shook my head in disbelief. I long suspected that the ravine itself would feel smaller on the day I came back to explore it as an adult. I was not disappointed. And I marveled at what my nine-year-old perceptions must have felt like. A sadness spread through me once more to remind me of what I had lost. I remembered a line from a poem that stayed with me like a song I couldn't get out of my head. The past, it said, was something we grieved more than what we longed to relive.

At last my morning trek through the ravine brought me to a sight I had not seen since Cliff and I were boyhood pioneers: I stood on the ravine's gentle slope on the south side of the home I lived in from the age of two until I moved away in my early twenties. I adored this house but its curb appeal paled compared to the view I took in now, framed by the colorful oak and beech and sugar maples I stood among.

The back of the house was the private side, a handsome, imposing facade. The peaked roof at the center of the building pointed up into the trees like the prow of a ship, reaching to touch the branches overhanging the yard. I was two hundred feet away, but certainly visible to anyone who lived there now if they had stood in front of one of the many windows facing the backyard.

Memories and voices and faces flooded my brain, and I froze, I could not move. My throat constricted again, and I felt tears course down my cheeks. The forest surrounded me but did not come to my rescue. I was overjoyed to finally be right here, and I was sad and hurting for all that I had left behind and never would be part of again.

And I was also grateful. Every window I stared at, although shielded by curtains, revealed to my memory a bedroom, a family room, a living room, a staircase whose every inch I had known. I was no longer a resident of this structure I knew so well. Today, I was a guest in a wooded theater, an audience of one, and the house and everything in it were now the setting and props on the stage of some other family's life.

Yet when I closed my eyes I saw not a play with other actors, but my own life re-enacted. I saw myself at twelve helping Dad pitch our canvas Coleman tent meant for ten people so that Cliff and I could camp out in the backyard.

"Pull the line taut," I could hear Dad say to me, "Good. Now push in the stake. All the way."

"Like this?"

"That's good."

We stood back and admired our work. Days later, when we took the tent down, the green grass beneath its footprint had turned a pale yellow.

Mike was shooting buckets on the patio with me in a game of twenty-one. The "whaap, whaap" of his bouncing basketball filled the backyard as if he were a marching drummer. His lefty jump shot arced high and clunked as it collided with the backboard, then whooshed through the net.

"Nice shot," I said.

Dad was standing on the balcony above the patio and photographing Jo in her prom gown, waiting for Jo's date to arrive. Dad snapped and Jo turned without being told to. They moved around in silence. Then in my mind I watched Dad down on the patio grilling burgers. He wore a Green Bay Packers polo shirt and black wingtips.

Mom, in khaki shorts, a floppy straw hat, and garden gloves, shears in her left hand, bent over her roses on the slope beneath the living-room windows, snipping buds on a warm June afternoon.

And Linda, riding the lawn mower around the backyard doing the chores I used to do before I'd left for college.

Flashes of memories, vivid, and fresh.

What an impossibly wonderful gift Mom and Dad had given me and Jo and Mike and Linda, a gift of security, comfort, opportunity. Here I was, standing in the mild fall weather of a Wisconsin October, a day away from laying Dad to rest, looking up at a home I have never relinquished entirely.

## 50

Irene made the only decision she could have made, the only decision she knew how to make on that day in 1956 when she declined Berlon's first proposal of marriage and chose instead to return to West Allis, Wisconsin to await my birth. There was nothing to forgive because I felt overwhelming gratitude for the gift she gave me.

I will never know Irene. At best I can say that drip by drip, memory by memory, my birth siblings have begun filling in the blanks that is the unfinished canvas of my birth mother.

What did I know about Mom, the woman who raised me? Certainly, more than I knew about Irene, but the blanks in my knowledge of Mom endure. Almost every time I speak to my sister Linda I discover some new facet of Mom's history, some new passion that occupied her, some obscure product she bought because she believed it was beneficial for the environment, someone else, a pregnant teen, a farm girl with few opportunities, who Mom believed needed her, needed us and she brought them into our fold.

The people we know best, have known the longest, remain mysteries. Linda knew more than I did about Mom. She also knew more about Dad, for whom she was a faithful caretaker and best friend, than I did. Proximity matters and Linda was there for Dad. I was not, at least not until his final fourteen months.

What would my birth siblings Susan, Jayne, Tony, John, and Chip say about the mother they lived with, grew up with, saw every day? They knew her, of course, hugged her, saw into her eyes, spoke to her. Would they acknowledge the mysteries, the secrets about her they still do not know, surrounding their mother? Chip tells me almost automatically, without thinking, "I have no memories of Momma." I think he has changed his mind.

If Irene were a crossword puzzle, she would be only 30 percent complete to me. I have her vital statistics, her height, weight, hair, and eye color. More than a few people have commented on her physical beauty.

Words were missing from the crossword puzzle of Irene. Even the clues were puzzles.

Mom had a gift for euphemism, her round-about path to a difficult truth. If I endured some loss or hardship, she'd try to comfort me by saying, "When it's your ox that's gored, it matters." I had to turn that one over in my head before I understood that the ox represented whatever injustice I felt I'd suffered. It wasn't her best effort, but she made me think. Mom and Irene each weathered hardship. Each withstood pain and loss. Each also knew joy and love, accomplishment, and pride.

Today, I am mindful that my gift to Mom was me. She and Dad tried to get pregnant and struggled. So they adopted. Professor Thurman defined waiting as the thing we do before we catapult to our next stage. He was talking about me.

Mom's gift to me, beyond the obvious love of a mother, was a devotion every child wrestles to comprehend. She never gave up on me.

I will never know Irene the way I knew Mom, yet both remain shrouded to me. The surprise, the happy serendipity, is that in letting go of the unknowable about Irene, I have discovered something I did not expect. Mom may have annoyed me, pushed my buttons, tried too hard to be a friend, but she was the author of my fondest childhood memories. Mom choreographed Santa's visit to our house on Christmas Eve and persuaded Mr. Mintz to play the lead role. Mom sent me and my siblings off to summer camp and Little League and Cub Scouts and basketball camp and a passel of other kid activities that confirmed how special I was (and we were) to two human beings who happened to have adopted me decades ago.

The most precious gift a mother—and a father—could bestow upon a child is mine forever. At any time, I can stop whatever I am doing and play back any one of thousands of memories from my childhood stored in a personal library in my brain (or is it my heart?). Are my memories richer or better than someone else's? It does not matter. This thing that I can do is available to everyone: the simple act of remembering.

What I know with certainty is that remembering is all that I need. Mom created a protective shield around our house—I could not see it, but I felt it—beginning with the ring of the brass bells that hung from the screen door in our garage and that called me home whenever I played in the ravine that surrounded our house. Those bells, which I can hear to this day, were for me like Mom's voice saying "If you hear the bells, you are safe. If you hear the bells, I am not far away."

Those brass bells were tuned as if for my ears only. Whenever I was playing deep in the ravine with my boyhood best friend Cliff and other chums and the high-pitched peal resonated in the air, only I turned in recognition.

"Hear that?" I'd say, standing up straight, head inclined a bit toward the faint but distinct sound in the distance.

"Hear what?" Cliff would say.

But I heard.

The bells were not a call for me to come home. They were a call to say I was already home.

Mom designed the house and the yards and the play spaces and the gardens, all of which were a child's haven. She was our private Walt Disney, inventing adventures, creating possibilities, opening doors, never giving up on any of us, and finding new and unexpected ways to say "I love you" in the best and only ways she knew how.

I did not see all of this clearly when she was alive, but now I do. I see Mom with beginner eyes. She is more whole to me today than at any time in my life. The best tribute I can pay to Irene is to say that the mother she gave me through the gift of adoption loved me the way I believe Irene would have loved me. I wish I had loved Mom more, knew her better, had asked her more about her life, but then I stop and realize one more thing, perhaps the most important thing of all. Love is never too late.

In searching for my birth mother, I found Mom.

Tony slowed his SUV and turned right onto a narrow, paved lane, then pulled over on the shoulder.

"This is it," he said, turning off the ignition. Drizzle blurred the windshield.

"The Jones Dairy?"

"Yessir."

Susan had come along with Tony and me on the last full day of my first visit to Nichols in December 2017. Nichols Highway curved around the old, decaying dairy farm.

"Not much to look at," said Susan.

"They gave it up in the sixties, I think," said Tony. "Hasn't been a working farm for decades."

"So it's just abandoned?" I asked.

"Lotta places around here are," said Tony.

I climbed out of Tony's SUV and walked around the vehicle until I was standing at the edge of the property. There was not much left. A beige and sandy-colored landscape, shells of two buildings, and a headless silo sagging under its own weight.

A light rain dampened my hair. Tony and Susan were silent. I watched them take in the scene, their heads swiveling slowly as if their eyes were movie cameras recording the moment. The crumbling buildings, I realized, were not what interested me. I turned and walked back toward Nichols Highway and stopped at the T intersection. Somewhere on this slight curve that hugged the small farm known as the Jones Dairy, George Watson's logging truck pummeled Junior's car, and in an instant...

In an instant, my life...

Reverend Michael had told me I existed in the mind of God before I was born and that I had chosen to be born, to "appear" in his words. It was my choice. Standing on this desolate spot, I had difficulty grasping Rev's idea. Maybe I was supposed to struggle. This, I think, was the point of letting go.

Irene and Berlon would not conceive me until weeks or months after the accident that took Junior's life. Right here. But on this ground, I could say that a new portal opened. For me.

I shook my head. I was facing away from Susan and Tony, so I don't think they saw me. Dull pinpricks of rain tickled my face.

Howard Thurman's words came back to me. "Fate is the raw materials of experience. They come uninvited and often unanticipated. Destiny is what a man does with these raw materials."

How often, I wondered, is a man given the privilege to stand on the ground where his fate emerged sixty years earlier? How often is a man blessed to stand on the ground sixty years later and reflect on where his destiny has led him?

## 52

Following dinner on the last evening before I returned to Los Angeles, nine months after I began this odyssey in March 2017, Susan and Tony had an idea, something they wanted me to see.

The three of us, plus Chip and Marianne, piled into Tony's SUV and drove a few miles until we reached a place they knew, but which seemed to me like another pasture left fallow. The night chill startled me, crisp and biting. We climbed out of the vehicle and walked a few paces onto the hardened ground. We huddled together.

And then I saw it, a sight I have not witnessed in decades. When you live in Los Angeles or any metropolis, a cloudless night sky is a lifeless, pale, insipid black. Light pollution breathes onto the unfocused dome as if it were a mirror misted over, blocking out the pinpricks of stars. If the moon has risen, it's almost the only object visible. Sometimes a planet peeks out. But rarely more than a few twinklers.

As our eyes adjusted, they were drawn upward, against our will. As if a presence placed a finger beneath our chins and lifted gently.

This sable sky pockmarked with white. A broad brushstroke

of light arced through the blackness like a sash of shimmering graffiti immersed in an inky ocean and slowly the tide retreated, leaving a watchful Milky Way.

We stood dumb beneath the beauty of the night sky. We could hear only our own breathing.

On cue, a single meteor sliced like a knife's edge across the horizon and vanished.

I stood in the field next to my sister, my two brothers, and a sister-in-law. Two days earlier they had welcomed me into their family home and their lives. Nine months before that I had never heard of them, and they knew little about me.

"No one will believe it," said Susan in barely more than a whisper.

# NOTES

**Chapter 2**
Verrier, Nancy Newton. *The Primal Wound: Understanding the Adopted Child*. Baltimore: Gateway Press, Inc., 1993.

**Chapter 4**
Ibid
Verrier, Nancy Newton. *Coming Home To Self: The Adopted Child Grows Up*. Baltimore: Gateway Press, Inc., 2003.

**Chapter 9**
Guide, Wisconsin Coastal. "Bluff Erosion in Ozaukee County." ArcGIS Story-Maps, May 27, 2022.

**Chapter 14**
Fessler, Ann. *The Girls Who Went Away: The Hidden History of Women Who Surrendered Children for Adoption in the Decades before Roe v. Wade*. New York: Penguin Books, 2006.

**Chapter 20**
Thurman, Howard. *For the Inward Journey: The Writings of Howard Thurman Selected by Anne Spencer Thurman*. Richmond, Indiana: Friends United Press, 1984.

**Chapter 28**
Thurman, Howard. *Essential Writings*. Ossinging, New York: Orbis Press, 2006.

**Chapter 34**
Bennard, George. *That Old Rugged Cross (Lyrics)*. 1912.

**Chapter 36**
Chodron, Pema. *When Things Fall Apart: Heart Advice for Difficult Times*. Boston: Shambala, 2000.

**Chapter 40**
Luscombe, Belinda. "10 Questions for Robert Caro." Time, May 21, 2012.
https://content.time.com/time/subscriber/article/0,33009,2114437,00.html

**Chapter 45**
O'Neill, Eugene. *A Moon for the Misbegotten*. Malmø Stadsteater, 1953.

**Chapter 48**
Grand, Ph.D, C.Psych, Michael Phillip. *The Adoption Constellation: New Ways of Thinking and Practicing Adoption*. 2010.
Verrier, Nancy Newton. *The Primal Wound: Understanding the Adopted Child*. Baltimore: Gateway Press, Inc., 1993.

**Chapter 51**
Thurman, Howard. *For the Inward Journey: The Writings of Howard Thurman Selected by Anne Spencer Thurman*. Richmond, Indiana: Friends United Press, 1984.

# ACKNOWLEDGMENTS

Adoption nomenclature has changed since I was a child. My adoptive parents are my parents. My birth family, which I used to refer to as my *biological family*, did not raise me so are not referred to as "parents" in this narrative.

Without the consent and support of my adoptive family, most especially my late father, Harold F. Ibach, I would have never considered undertaking either the search for my birth family nor writing about it. I believe my late mother, Martha Joyce, would have approved as well.

I am indebted to my sister Mary Jo, who first informed me about Wisconsin's laws, and encouraged me to take advantage. As an adoptee, she wanted me to join her in her search. I know she wanted a partner with whom to share notes and stories. We did this together.

I feel a deep love for and gratitude toward my sister Linda for her friendship, support and counsel.

To Susan, Jayne, Tony, and Chip: Thank you for helping me tell your story. To Marianne: Your Christmas kitchen reminds me of home.

To John: Someday, brother, we'll meet.

To my brothers and sisters at InsideOUT Writers Alumni Writing Circle in Los Angeles, who heard early drafts of some of the chapters that comprise this memoir, you are too many to name, but you know who you are. These are remarkable young men and women, all formerly incarcerated, all unique beings and confident voices who shared their life stories on Thursday nights in the safe space of IOW. They gave me courage and a deep sense of belonging. You cannot know how much you mean to me.

To Rose Safran, who nudged me to take this journey and stood with me.

To Kerry Lenzendorf, adoption specialist in the Department of Families in Wisconsin: Thank you for opening the door and helping me shed light on what has been hidden for so long.

To Reverend Dr. Michael Bernard Beckwith, founder and spiritual director of Agape International Spiritual Center, my friend and teacher. Thank you for the title of this book. One of many acorns you've bestowed upon me.

To Leslie Schwartz, my editor, guide, and friend, I express my gratitude for your experienced hand in helping me turn a tossed salad of a manuscript into this story.

To Crystal Durnan, Wanja Hubert, Don Johnson, and Shirley Drow for their keen eyes, astute critiques and support on my long journey: I am grateful.

Finally, but not least, to novelist and retired United States Air Force Colonel Noel Zamot, my writing confidant: You never know what might happen when you invite a stranger to join you and your family for dessert at a restaurant in Rome on Thanksgiving night. In profound gratitude.

# MY FAMLIES

**My adoptive family**
Harold Frederick Ibach, father (1926 – 2022)
Martha Joyce Mendenhall Ibach, mother (1927 – 2008)
Howard Frederick Ibach, author (1956 – )
Mary Jo Ibach, sister (1958 – ; also adopted, but from a different birth mother)
Suzanne Esther Ibach, sister (January 4, 1960 – January 6, 1960) [my adoptive parents' first biological child]
Michael John Ibach, brother (1961 – 1980; my adoptive parents' second biological child)
Linda Mendenhall Ibach, sister (1962 – ; my adoptive parents' third biological child)
Herbert Frederick Ibach, paternal grandfather (1889 – 1969)
Belva Rohrer Ibach, paternal grandmother (1895 – 1991)
Ernest Albert Mendenhall, maternal grandfather (1901 – 1982)
Edna Clark Mendenhall, maternal grandmother (1904 – 1991)

**My birth family**
> Irene Lucile Manousos McCrackin, mother (1929 – 1976)
> Berlon McCrackin, father (1926 – 2003)
> Susan Small McCrackin, half-sister (1953 – )
> Jayne Small McCrackin, half-sister (1955 – )
> David Small, author (1956 – )
> Tony McCrackin, brother (1961 – )
> John McCrackin, brother (1962 – )
> Chip McCrackin, brother (1964 – )

# ABOUT THE AUTHOR

Howard Frederick Ibach was raised in Milwaukee, Wisconsin. He earned degrees at the University of Tampa and Brown University. For twenty-six years, he was an advertising copywriter and creative director, and now is an instructor for the Association of National Advertisers' Marketing Training and Development Center. Ibach lives in Southern California and is at work on a new memoir.